Ballads and Barrack-room Ballads

Rudyard Kipling

Contents

BALLADS AND
BARRACK-ROOM BALLADS

BY

Rudyard Kipling

THE BALLAD OF EAST AND WEST

Oh, East is East, and West is West, and never the twain shall meet,
Till Earth and Sky stand presently at God's great Judgment Seat;
But there is neither East nor West, Border, nor Breed, nor Birth,
When two strong men stand face to face, tho' they come from the
ends of the earth !

Kamal is out with twenty men to raise the Border side,
And he has lifted the Coloners mare that is the Colonel's pride:
He has lifted her out of the stable-door between the dawn and the day,
And turned the calkins upon her feet, and ridden her far away.

Then up and spoke the Colonel's son that led a troop of the Guides:
'Is there never a man of all my men can say where Kamal hides?'
Then up and spoke Mahommed Khan, the son of the Ressaldar,
'If ye know the track of the morning-mist, ye know where his pickets are.
'At dusk he harries the Abazai—at dawn he is into Bonair,
'But he must go by Fort Bukloh to his own place to fare,
'So if ye gallop to Fort Bukloh as fast as a bird can
'By the fayour of God ye may cut him off ere he win to the Tongue of Jagai,
'But if he be passed the Tongue of Jagai, right swiftly turn ye then,
'For the length and the breadth of that grisly plain is sown with Kamal's men.
'There is rock to the left, and rock to the right, and low lean thorn between,
'And ye may hear a breech-bolt snick where never a man is seen.'

The Colonel,s son has taken a horse, and a raw rough dun was he,

With the mouth of a bell and the heart of Hell, and the head of the gallows-
tree.
The Colonel's son to the Fort has won, they bid him stay to eat—
Who rides at the tail of a Border thief, he sits not long at his meat.
He's up and away from Fort Bukloh as fast as he can fly,
Till he was aware of his father's mare in the gut of the Tongue of Jagai,
Till he was aware of his father's mare with Kamal upon her back,
And when he could spy the white of her eye, he made the pistol crack.
He has fired once, he has fired twice, but the whist-ling ball went wide.
'Ye shoot like a soldier! Kamal said. 'Show now if ye can ride.'
It's up and over the Tongue of Jagai, as blown dust-devils go,
The dun he fled like a stag of ten, but the mare like a barren doe.

The dun he leaned against the bit and slugged his head above,
But the red mare played with the snaffle-bars, as a maiden plays with a glove.
There was rock to the left and rock to the right, and low lean thorn between,
And thrice he heard a breech-bolt snick tho' never a man was seen.
They have ridden the low moon out of the sky, their hoofs drum up the dawn,
The dun he went like a wounded bull, but the mare like a new-roused fawn.
The dun he fell at a water-course—in a woful heap fell he,
And Kamal has turned the red mare back, and pulled the rider free.
He has knocked the pistol out of his hand—small room was there to strive,
"Twas only by favour of mine,' quoth he, 'ye rode so long alive:
'There was not a rock for twenty mile, there was not a clump of tree,
'But covered a man of my own men with his rifle cocked on his knee.
'If I had raised my bridle-hand, as I have held it low,
'The little jackals that flee so fast, were feasting all in a row:
'If I had bowed my head on my breast, as I have held it high,
'The kite that whistles above us now were gorged till she could not fly.'
Lightly answered the Colonel's son:—'Do good to bird and beast,
'But count who come for the broken meats before thou makest a feast.
'If there should follow a thousand swords to carry my bones away,
'Belike the price of a jackal's meal were more than a thief could pay.

'They will feed their horse on the standing crop, their men on the garnered grain,
'The thatch of the byres will serve their fires when all the cattle are slain.
'But if hou thinkest the price be fair,—thy brethren wait to sup,
'The hound is kin to the jackal-spawn,—howl, dog, and call them up!

'And if thou thinkest the price be high, in steer and gear and stack,
'Give me my father's mare again, and I'll fight my own way back!'
Kamal has gripped him by the hand and set him upon his feet.
'No talk shall be of dogs/ said he, 'when wolf and grey wolf meet.
'May I eat dirt if thou hast hurt of me in deed or breath;
'What dam of lances brought thee forth to jest at the dawn with Death?'
Lightly answered the Colonel's son: 'I hold by the blood of my clan :
'Take up the mare for my father's gift—by God, she has carried a man!'
The red mare ran to the Colonel's son, and nuzzled against his breast,
'We be two strong men,' said Kamal then, 'but she loveth the younger best.
'So she shall go with a lifter's dower, my turquoise-studded rein,
'My broidered saddle and saddle-cloth, and silver stirrups twain.'

The Colonel's son a pistol drew and held it muzzle-end,
'Ye have taken the one from a foe/ said he; 'will ye take the mate from a friend ?'
'A gift for a gift,' said Kamal straight; 'a limb for the risk of a limb.
'Thy father has sent his son to me, I'll send my son to him!'
With that he whistled his only son, that dropped from a mountain-crest—
He trod the ling like a buck in spring, and he looked like a lance in rest.
'Now here is thy master,' Kamal said, 'who leads a troop of the Guides,
'And thou must ride at his left side. as shield on shoulder rides.
'Till Death or I cut loose the tie, at camp and board and bed,
'Thy life is his—thy fate it is to guard him with thy head.
'So thou must eat the White Queen's meat, and all her foes are thine,
'And thou must harry thy father's hold for the peace of the Border-line,
'And thou must make a trooper tough and hack thy way to power—

'Belike they will raise thee to Ressaldar when I am hanged in Peshawur.'

They have looked each other between the eyes, and there they found no fault,
They have taken the Oath of the Brother-in-Blood on leavened bread and salt:
They have taken the Oath of the Brother-in-Blood on fire and fresh-cut sod,
On the hilt and the haft of the Khyber knife, and the Wondrous Names of God.
The Coloners son he rides the mare and Kamal's boy the dun,
And two have come back to Fort Bukloh where there went forth but one.
And when they drew to the Quarter-Guard, full twenty swords flew clear—
There was not a man but carried his feud with the blood of the mountaineer.
'Ha' done! ha' done!' said the Colonel's son.
'Put up the steel at your sides!

'Last night ye had struck at a Border thief—tonight 'tis a man of the Guides!'

Oh, East is East, and West is West, and never the two shall meet,
Till Earth and Sky stand presently at God's great Judgment Seat;
But there is neither East nor West, Border, nor Breed, nor Birth,
When two strong men stand face to face, tho' they come from the ends of the
earth.

THE LAST SUTTEE

Not many years ago a King died in one of the Rajpoot States. His wives, dis-
regarding the orders of the English against suttee, would have broken out of the
palace had not the gates been barred. But one of them, disguised as the icing's
favourite dancing-girl, passed through the line of guards and reached the pyre.
There; her courage fail-ing, she prayed her cousin, a baron of the court, to kill
her. This he did, not knowing who she was.

UDAI CHAND lay sick to death
In his hold by Gungra hill.

All night we heard the death-gongs ring
For the soul of the dying Rajpoot King,
All night beat up from the women's wing
A cry that we could not still.

All night the barons came and went,
The lords of the outer guard:
All night the cressets glimmered pale
On Ulwar sabre and Tonk jezail,
Mewar headstall and Marwar mail,
That clinked in the palace yard.

In the Golden room on the palace roof
All night he fought for air:
And there was sobbing behind the screen,
Rustle and whisper of women unseen,
And the hungry eyes of the Boondi Queen
On the death she might not share.

He passed St dawn—the death-fire leaped
From ridge to river-head,
From the Malwa plains to the Abu scaurs:
And wail upon wail went up to the stars
Behind the grim zenana-bars,
When they knew that the King was dead.

The dumb priest knelt to tie his mouth
And robe him for the pyre.
The Boondi Queen beneath us cried:
'See, now, that we die as our mothers died
'In the bridal-bed by our master's side!
'Out, women!—to the fire!'

We drove the great gates home apace:
White hands were on the sill:
But ere the rush of the unseen feet
Had reached the turn to the open street,
The bars shot down, the guard-drum beat—
We held the dove-cot still.

A face looked down in the gathering day,
And laughing spoke from the wall:
'Ohe, they mourn here: let me b—
'Azizun, the Lucknow nautch-girl, I?
'When the house is rotten, the rats must fly,
'And I seek another thrall.

'For I ruled the King as ne'er did Queen,—
'To-night the Queens rule me!
'Guard them safely, but let me go,
'Or ever they pay the debt they owe
'In scourge and torture!' She leaped below,
And the grim guard watched her flee.

They knew that the King had spent his soul
On a North-bred dancing-girl:
That he prayed to a flat-nosed Lucknow god,
And kissed the ground where her feet had trod,
And doomed to death at her drunken nod
And swore by her lightest curl.

We bore the King to his fathers' place,
Where the tombs of the Sun-born stand:
Where the grey apes swing, and the peacocks preen
On fretted pillar and jewelled screen,
And the wild boar couch in the house of the Queen

On the drift of the desert sand.

The herald read his titles forth,
We set the logs aglow:
' Friend of the English, free from fear,
'Baron of Luni to Jeysulmeer,
'Lord of the Desert of Bikaneer,
'King of the Jungle,—go!'

All night the red flame stabbed the sky
With wavering wind-tossed spears:
And out of a shattered temple crept
A woman who veiled her head and wept,
And called on the King—but the great King slept,
And turned not for her tears.

Small thought had he to mark the strife—
Cold fear with hot desire—
When thrice she leaped from the leaping flame,
And thrice she beat her breast for shame,
And thrice like a wounded dove she came
And moaned about the fire.

One watched, a bow-shot from the blaze,
The silent streets between,
Who had stood by the King in sport and fray,
To blade in ambush or boar at bay,
And he was a baron old and grey,
And kin to the Boondi Queen.

He said: 'O shameless, put aside
'The veil upon thy brow!
'Who held the King and all his land

'To the wanton will of a harlot's hand!
'Will the white ash rise from the blistered brand?
'Stoop down, and call him now!'

Then she: 'By the faith of my tarnished soul,
'All things I did not well
'I had hoped to clear ere the fire died,
'And lay me down by my master's side
'To rule in Heaven his only bride,
'While the others howl in Hell.

'But I have felt the fire's breath,
'And hard it is to die!
'Yet if I may pray a Rajpoot lord
'To sully the steel of a Thakur's sword
'With base-born blood of a trade abhorred,'—
And the Thakur answered, 'Ay.'

He drew and struck: the straight blade drank
The life beneath the breast.
'I had looked for the Queen to face the flame
'But the harlot dies for the Rajpoot dame—
'Sister of mine, pass, free from shame.
'Pass with thy King to rest!'

The black log crashed above the white:
The little flames and lean,
Red as slaughter and blue as steel,
That whistled and fluttered from head to heel
Leaped up anew, for they found their meal
On the heart of—the Boondi Queen!

THE BALLAD OF THE KING'S MERCY

Abdhur Rahman, the Durani Chief, of him is the story told.
His mercy fills the Khyber hills—his grace is manifold;
He has taken toll of the North and the South—his glory reacheth far,
And they tell the tale of his charity from Balkh to Kandahar.

Before the old Peshawur Gate, where Kurd and Kaffir meet,
The Governor of Kabul dealt the Justice of the Street
And that was strait as running noose and swift as plunging knife,
Tho he who held the longer purse might hold the longer life.

There was a hound of Hindustan had struck a Euzufzai,
Wherefore they spat upon his face and led him out to die.
It chanced the King went forth that hour when throat was bared to knife;
The Kaffir grovelled under-hoof and clamoured for his life.

Then said the King: 'Have hope, O friend! Yea, Death disgraced is hard;
'Much honour shall be thine '; and called the Captain of the Guard,
Yar Khan, a bastard of the Blood, so city-babble saith,
And he was honoured of the King—the which is salt to Death;
And he was son of Daoud Shah the Reiver of the Plains,
And blood of old Durani Lords ran fire in his veins;
And 'twas to tame an Afghan pride nor Hell nor Heaven could bind,
The King would make him butcher to a yelping cur of Hind.

'Strike!' said the King. 'King's blood art thou— his death shall be his pride!'
Then louder, that the crowd might catch: 'Fear not—his arms are tied!'
Yar Khan drew clear the Khyber knife, and struck, and sheathed again.
'O man, thy will is done,' quoth he; 'A King this dog hath slain.'

Abdhur Rahman, the Durani Chief, to the North and the South is sold.
The North and the South shall open their mouth to a Ghilzai flag unrolled,
When the big guns speak to the Khyber peak, and his dog-Heratis fly,

Ye have heard the song — How long? How long? Wolves of the Abazai!

That night before the watch was set, when all the streets were clear,
The Governor of Kabul spoke: 'My King, hast thou no fear?
'Thou knowest—thou hast heard,'—his speech died at his master's face.

And grimly said the Afghan King: 'I rule the Afghan race.
'My path is mine—see thou to thine—to-night upon thy bed
'Think who there be in Kabul now that clamour for thy head. '

That night when all the gates were shut to City and to Throne,
Within a little garden-house the King lay down alone.
Before the sinking of the moon, which is the Night of Night,
Yar Khan came softly to the King to make his honour white.
The children of the town had mocked beneath his horse's hoofs,
The harlots of the town had hailed him 'butcher!' from their roofs.
But as he groped against the wall, two hands upon him fell,
The King behind his shoulder spoke: 'Dead man, thou dost not well!

"Tis ill to jest with Kings by day and seek a boon by night;
'And that thou bearest in thy hand is all too sharp to write.
'But three days hence, if God be good, and if thy strength remain,
'Thou shalt demand one boon of me and bless me in thy pain.
'For I am merciful to all, and most of all to thee.
'My butcher of the shambles, rest—no knife hast thou for me!'

Abdhur Rahman, the Durani Chief, holds hard by the South and the North;
But the Ghilzai knows, ere the melting snows, when the swollen banks break forth,
When the red-coats crawl to the sungar wall, and his Usbeg lances fail.
Ye have heard the song—How long? How long? Wolves of the Zuka Kheyl!

They stoned him in the rubbish-field when dawn was in the sky,

According to the written word, 'See that he do not die.'
They stoned him till the stones were piled above him on the plain,
And those the labouring limbs displaced they tumbled back again.

One watched beside the dreary mound that veiled the battered thing,
And him the King with laughter called the Herald of the King.
It was upon the second night, the night of Ramazan,
The watcher leaning earthward heard the message of Yar Khan.
From shattered breast through shrivelled lips broke forth the rattling breath:
'Creature of God, deliver me from agony of Death.'
They sought the King among his girls, and risked their lives thereby:
'Protector of the Pitiful, give orders that he die!'

'Bid him endure until the day,' a lagging answer came;
'The night is short, and he can pray and learn to bless my name. '
Before the dawn three times he spoke, and on the day once more:
'Creature of God, deliver me and bless the King therefore!'
They shot him at the morning prayer, to ease him of his pain,
And when he heard the matchlocks clink, he blessed the King again.
Which thing the singers made a song for all the world to sing,
So that the Outer Seas may know the mercy of the King.

Abdhur Rahman, the Durani Chief of him is the story told.
He has opened his mouth to the North and the South, they have stuffed his
mouth with gold.
Ye know the truth of his tender ruth—and sweet his favours are.
Ye have heard the song—How long? How long? from Balkh to Kandahar.

THE BALLAD OF THE KING'S JEST

WHEN spring-time flushes the desert grass,
Our kafilas wind through the Khyber Pass.

Lean are the camels but fat the frails,
Light are the purses but heavy the bales,
As the snowbound trade of the North comes down
To the market-square of Peshawur town.

In a turquoise twilight, crisp and chill,
A kafila camped at the foot of the hill.
Then blue smoke-haze of the cooking rose,
And tentpeg answered to hammer-nose;
And the picketed ponies shag and wild,
Strained at their ropes as the feed was piled;
And the bubbling camels beside the load
Sprawled for a furlong adown the road;
And the Persian pussy-cats, brought for sale,
Spat at the dogs from the camel-bale;
And the tribesmen bellowed to hasten the food;

And the camp-fires twinkled by Fort Jumrood;
And there fled on the wings of the gathering dusk
 A savour of camels and carpets and musk,
A murmur of voices, a reek of smoke,
To tell us the trade of the Khyber woke.

The lid of the flesh-pot chattered high,
The knives were whetted and—then came I
To Mahbub Ali, the muleteer,
Patching his bridles and counting his gear,
Crammed with the gossip of half a year.
But Mahbub Ali the kindly said,
'Better is speech when the belly is'fed.'
So we plunged the hand to the mid-wrist deep
In a cinnamon stew of the fat-tailed sheep,
And he who never hath tasted the food,

By Allah! he knoweth not bad from good.

We cleansed our beards of the mutton-grease,
We lay on the mats and were filled with peace,
And the talk slid north, and the talk slid south,
With the sliding puffs from the hookah-mouth.
Four things greater than all things are, —
Women and Horses and Power and War.
We spake of them all, but the last the most,

For I sought a word of a Russian post,-
Of a shifty promise, an unsheathed sword
And a grey-coat guard on the Helmund ford.
Then Mahbub Ali lowered his eyes
In the fashion of one who is weaving lies.
Quoth he: 'Of the Russians who can say?
'When the night is gathering all is grey.
'But we look that the gloom of the night shall die
'In the morning flush of a blood-red sky.
'Friend of my heart, is it meet or wise
'To warn a King of his enemies?
'We know what Heaven or Hell may bring,
'But no man knoweth the mind of the King.
'That unsought counsel is cursed of God
'Attesteth the story of Wali Dad.

' His sire was leaky of tongue and pen,
' His dam was a clucking Khuttuck hen;
' And the colt bred close to the vice of each,
' For he carried the curse of an unstaunched speech.
' Therewith madness — so that he sought
' The favour of kings at the Kabul court;
' And travelled, in hope of honour, far

'To the line where the grey-coat squadrons are.
'There have I journeyed too — but I

'Saw naught, said naught, and—did not die!
'He hearked to rumour, and snatched at a breath
'Of "this one knoweth" and "that one saith,"—
'Legends that ran from mouth to mouth
'Of a grey-coat coming, and sack of the South.
'These have I also heard—they pass
'With each new spring and the winter grass.

'Hot-foot southward, forgotten of God,
'Back to the city ran Wali Dad,
'Even to Kabul—in full durbar
'The King held talk with his Chief in War.
'Into the press of the crowd he broke,
'And what he had heard of the coming spoke.

'Then Gholam Hyder, the Red Chief, smiled,
'As a mother might on a babbling child;
'But those who would laugh restrained their breath,
'When the face of the King showed dark as death.
'Evil it is in full durbar
'To cry to a ruler of gathering war!
'Slowly he led to a peach-tree small,
'That grew by a cleft of the city wall.
'And he said to the boy: "They shall praise thy zeal
'"So long as the red spurt follows the steel.

'"And the Russ is upon us even now?
'"Great is thy prudence—await them, thou.
'"Watch from the tree. Thou art young and strong,
'"Surely thy vigil is not for long.

'"The Russ is upon us, thy clamour ran?
'"Surely an hour shall bring their van.
'"Wait and watch. When the host is near,
'"Shout aloud that my men may hear."

'Friend of my heart, is it meet or wise
'To warn a King of his enemies?
'A guard was set that he might not flee—
'A score of bayonets ringed the tree.
'The peach-bloom fell in showers of snow,
'When he shook at his death as he looked below.
'By the power of God, who alone is great,
'Till the seventh day he fought with his fate.
'Then madness took him, and men declare
'He mowed in the branches as ape and bear,
'And last as a sloth, ere his body failed,
'And he hung as a bat in the forks, and wailed,
'And sleep the cord of his hands untied,
'And he fell, and was caught on the points and died.

'Heart of my heart, is it meet or wise
'To warn a King of his enemies?
'We know what Heaven or Hell may bring,
'But no man knoweth the mind of the King.
'Of the grey-coat coming who can say?
'When the night is gathering all is grey.
'Two things greater than all things are,
'The first is Love, and the second War.
'And since we know not how War may prove,
'Heart of my heart, let us talk of Love!'

WITH SCINDIA TO DELHI

More than a hundred years ago, in a great battle fought near Delhi, an Indian Prince rode fifty miles after the day was lost with a beggar-girl, who had loved him and followed him in all his camps, on his saddle-bow. He lost the girl when almost within sight of safety. A Maratta trooper tells the story: —

THE wreath of banquet overnight lay withered on the neck,
Our hands and scarves were saffron-dyed for signal of despair,
When we went forth to Paniput to battle with the ***Mlech,*** —
Ere we came back from Paniput and left a kingdom there.
Thrice thirty-thousand men were we to force the Jumna fords—
The hawk-winged horse of Damajee, mailed squadrons of the Bhao,
Stark levies of the southern hills, the Deccan's sharpest swords,
And he the harlot's traitor son the goatherd Mulhar Rao!

Thrice thirty-thousand men were we before the mists had cleared,
The low white mists of morning heard the war-conch scream and bray;
We called upon Bhowani and we gripped them by the beard,
We rolled upon them like a flood and washed their ranks away.

The children of the hills of Khost before our lances ran,
We drove the black Rohillas back as cattle to the pen;
'Twas then we needed Mulhar Rao to end what we began,
A thousand men had saved the charge; he fled the field with ten!

There was no room to clear a sword—no power to strike a blow,
For foot to foot, ay, breast to breast, the battle held us fast—
Save where the naked hill men ran and stabbing from below
Brought down the horse and rider and we trampled them and passed.

To left the roar of musketry rang like a falling flood-

To right the sunshine rippled red from redder lance and blade—
Above the dark Upsaras [1] flew, beneath us plashed the blood,
And, bellying black against the dust, the Bhagwa Jhanda swayed.

I saw it fall in smoke and fire, the banner of the Bhao;
I heard a voice across the press of one who called in vain:—

[1]The Choosers of the Slain.

'Ho! Anand Rao Nimbalkhur ride! Get aid of Mulhar Rao!
'Go shame his squadrons into fight—the Bhao— the Bhao is slain!'

Thereat, as when a sand-bar breaks in clotted spume and spray—
When rain of later autumn sweeps the Jumna water-head,
Before their charge from flank to flank our riven ranks gave way;
But of the waters of that flood the Jumna fords ran red.

I held by Scindia, my lord, as close as man might hold;
A Soobah of the Deccan asks no aid to guard his life;
But Holkar's Horse were flying, and our chief est chiefs were cold,
And like a flame among us leapt the long lean Northern knife.

I held by Scindia—my lance from butt to tuft was dyed,
The froth of battle bossed the shield and roped the bridle-chain—
What time beneath our horses' feet a maiden rose and cried,
And clung to Scindia, and I turned a sword-cut from the twain.

(He set a spell upon the maid in woodlands long ago,
A hunter by the Tapti banks she gave him water there:
He turned her heart to water, and she followed to her woe.
What need had he of Lalun who had twenty maids as fair?)

Now in that hour strength left my lord; he wrenched his mare aside;

He bound the girl behind him and we slashed and struggled free.
Across the reeling wreck of strife we rode as shadows ride
From Paniput to Delhi town, but not alone were we.

'Twas Lutuf-Ullah Populzai laid horse upon our track,
A swine-fed reiver of the North that lusted for the maid;
I might have barred his path awhile, but Scindia called me back,
And I—Oh woe for Scindia!—I listened and obeyed.

League after league the formless scrub took shape and glided by—
League after league the white road swirled behind the white mare's feet—
League after league, when leagues were done, we heard the Populzai,
Where sure as Time and swift as Death the tireless footfall beat.

"Noon's eye beheld that shame of flight, the shadows fell, we fled
Where steadfast as the wheeling kite he followed in our train;
The black wolf warred where we had warred, the jackal mocked our dead,
And terror born of twilight tide made mad the labouring brain.

I gasped:—'A kingdom waits my lord; her love is but her own.
'A day shall mar, a day shall cure for her, but what for thee ?
'Cut loose the girl: he follows fast. Cut loose and ride alone!'
Then Scindia 'twixt his blistered lips:—'My Queens' Queen shall she be!

'Of all who eat my bread last night 'twas she alone that came
'To seek her love between the spears and find her crown therein!
'One shame is mine to-day, what need the weight of double shame?
'If once we reach the Delhi gate, though all be lost, I win!'

We rode—the white mare failed—her trot a staggering stumble grew,—
The cooking-smoke of even rose and weltered and hung low;
And still we heard the Populzai and still we strained anew,
And Delhi town was very near, but nearer was the foe.

Yea, Delhi town was very near when Lalun whispered: —'Slay!
'Lord of my life, the mare sinks fast—stab deep and let me die!'
But Scindia would not, and the maid tore free and flung away,
And turning as she fell we heard the clattering Populzai.

Then Scindia checked the gasping mare that rocked and groaned for breath,
And wheeled to charge and plunged the knife a hands-breadth in her side—
The hunter and the hunted know how that last pause is death—
The blood had chilled about her heart, she reared and fell and died.

Our Gods were kind. Before he heard the maiden's piteous scream
A log upon the Delhi road, beneath the mare he lay—
Lost mistress and lost battle passed before him like a dream;
The darkness closed about his eyes—I bore my King away.

THE BALLAD OF BOH DA THONE

This is the ballad of Boh Da Thone,
Erst a Pretender to Theebaw's throne,
Who harried the district of Alalone:
How he met with his fate and the V.PP.
At the hand of Harendra Mukerji,
Senior Gomashta, G.B.T.

Boh Da Thone was a warrior bold,
His sword and his Snider were bossed with gold,

And the Peacock Banner his henchmen bore
Was stiff with bullion but stiffer with gore.

He shot at the strong and he slashed at the weak

From the Salween scrub to the Chindwin teak:

He crucified noble, he sacrificed mean,
He filled old women with kerosene:

While over the water the papers cried,
'The patriot fights for his countryside!'

But little they cared for the Native Press,
The worn white soldiers in Khaki dress,

Who tramped through the jungle and camped in the byre,
Who died in the swamp and were tombed in the mire,

Who gave up their lives, at the Queen's Command,
For the Pride of their Race and the Peace of the Land.

Now, first of the foemen of Boh Da Thone
Was Captain O'Neil of the 'Black Tyrone,'

And his was a Company, seventy strong,
Who hustled that dissolute Chief along.

There were lads from Galway and Louth and Meath
Who went to their death with a joke in their teeth,

And worshipped with fluency, fervour, and zeal
The mud on the boot-heels of 'Crook' O'Neil.

But ever a blight on their labours lay,
And ever their quarry would vanish away,

Till the sun-dried boys of the Black Tyrone

Took a brotherly interest in Boh Da Thone:

And, sooth, if pursuit in possession ends,
The Boh and his trackers were best of friends.

The word of a scout—a march by night—
A rush through the mist—a scattering fight—

A volley from cover—a corpse in the clearing—
The glimpse of a loin-cloth and heavy jade earring—

The flare of a village—the tally of slain—
And ... the Boh was abroad 'on the raid ' again!

They cursed their luck as the Irish will,
They gave him credit for cunning and skill,

They buried their dead, they bolted their beef,
And started anew on the track of the thief

Till, in place of the 'Kalends of Greece,' men said,
'When Crook and his darlings come back with the head.'

They had hunted the Boh from the Hills to the plain—
He doubled and broke for the hills again:

They had crippled his power for rapine and raid,
They had routed him out of his pet stockade,

And at last, they came, when the Day Star tired,
To a camp deserted—a village fired.

A black cross blistered the Morning-gold,

And the body upon it was stark and cold.

The wind of the dawn went merrily past,
The high grass bowed her plumes to the blast.
And out of the grass, on a sudden, broke
A spirtle of fire, a whorl of smoke—

And Captain O'Neil of the Black Tyrone
Was blessed with a slug in the ulna-bone—
The gift of his enemy Boh Da Thone.

(Now a slug that is hammered from telegraph-wire
Is a thorn in the flesh and a rankling fire.)

The shot-wound festeied—as shot-wounds may
In a steaming barrack at Mandalay.

The left arm throbbed, and the Captain swore,
'I'd like to be after the Boh once morel'

The fever held him—the Captain said,
'I'd give a hundred to look at his head!'

The Hospital punkahs creaked and whirred,
But Babu Harendra (Gomashta) heard.

He thought of the cane-brake, green and dank,
That girdled his home by the Dacca tank.

He thought of his wife and his High School son,
He thought—but abandoned the thought—of a gun.

His sleep was broken by visions dread

Of a shining Boh with a silver head.

He kept his counsel and went his way,
And swindled the cartmen of half their pay.

And the months went on, as the worst must do,
And the Boh returned to the raid anew.

But the Captain had quitted the long-drawn strife,
And in far Simoorie had taken a wife.

And she was a damsel of delicate mould,
With hair like the sunshine and heart of gold,

And little she knew the arms that embraced
Had cloven a man from the brow to the waist:

And little she knew that the loving lips
Had ordered a quivering life's eclipse,

And the eye that lit at her lightest breath
Had glared unawed in the Gates of Death.

(For these be matters a man would hide,
As a general rule, from an innocent Bride.)

And little the Captain thought of the past,
And, of all men, Babu Harendra last

But slow, in the sludge of the Kathun road,
The Government Bullock Train toted its load.

Speckless and spotless and shining with *ghee*,

In the rearmost cart sat the Babu-jee.

And ever a phantom before him fled
Of a scowling Boh with a silver head.

Then the lead-cart stuck, though the coolies slaved,
And the cartmen flogged and the escort raved;

And out of the jungle, with yells and squeals,
Pranced Boh Da Thone, and his gang at his heels!

Then belching blunderbuss answered back
The Snider's snarl and the carbine's crack,

And the blithe revolver began to sing
To the blade that twanged on the locking-ring,

And the brown flesh blued where the bay'net
kissed,
As the steel shot back with a wrench and a twist,

And the great white bullocks with onyx eyes
Watched the souls of the dead arise,

And over the smoke of the fusillade
The Peacock Banner staggered and swayed,

Oh, gayest of scrimmages man may see
Is a well-worked rush on the G.B.T.!

The Babu shook at the horrible sight,
And girded his ponderous loins for flight,

But Fate had ordained that the Boh should start
On a lone-hand raid of the rearmost cart,

And out of that cart, with a bellow of woe,
The Babu fell—flat on the top of the Boh!

For years had Harendra served the State,
To the growth of his purse and the girth of his *pit* —

There were twenty stone, as the tally-man knows,
On the broad of the chest of this best of Bohs.

And twenty stone from a height discharged
Are bad for a Boh with a spleen enlarged.

Oh, short was the struggle—severe was the shock—
He dropped like a bullock—he lay like a block;

And the Babu above him, convulsed with fear,
Heard the labouring life-breath hissed out in his ear.

And thus in a fashion undignified
The princely pest of the Chindwin died.

Turn now to Simoorie where, lapped in his ease,
The Captain is petting the Bride on his knees,

Where the *whit* of the bullet, the wounded man's Scream
Are mixed as the mist of some devilish dream—

Forgotten, forgotten the sweat of the shambles
Where the hill-daisy blooms and the grey monkey gambols,

From the sword-belt set free and released from the steel,
The Peace of the Lord is with Captain O'Neil.

Up the hill to Simoorie—most patient of drudges—
The bags on his shoulder, the mail-runner trudges.

'For Captain O'Neil, Sahib. One hundred and ten Rupees to collect on delivery.'

Then
(Their breakfast was stopped while the screw-jack and hammer
Tore wax-cloth, split teak-wood, and chipped out the dammer;)

Open-eyed, open-mouthed, on the napery's snow,
With a crash and a thud, rolled—the Head of the Boh!

And gummed to the scalp was a letter which ran:—

'IN FIELDING FORCE SERVICE. '*Encampment,*

'Ioth Jan.

'Dear Sir,— I have honour to send, *as you said,*
'For final approval (see under) Boh's Head;

'Was took by myself in most bloody affair.
'By High Education brought pressure to bear.

'Now violate Liberty, time being bad,
'To mail V.P.P. (rupees hundred) Please add

'Whatever Your Honour can pass. Price of Blood
'Much cheap at one hundred, and children want food.

'So trusting Your Honour will somewhat retain
'True love and affection for Govt. Bullock Train,

'And show awful kindness to satisfy me,

'I am,
'Graceful Master,
'Your
'H, Mukerji.'

As the rabbit is drawn to the rattlesnake's power,
As the smoker's eye fills at the opium hour,

As a horse reaches up to the manger above,
As the waiting ear yearns for the whisper of love,

From the arms of the Bride, iron-visaged and slow,
The Captain bent down to the Head of the Boh.

And e'en as he looked on the Thing where It lay
'Twixt the winking new spoons and the napkins' array,

The freed mind fled back to the long-ago days—
The hand-to-hand scuffle—the smoke and the blaze—

The forced march at night and the quick rush at dawn—
The banjo at twilight, the burial ere morn—

The stench of the marshes—the raw, piercing smell
When the overhand stabbing-cut silenced the yell—

The oaths of his Irish that surged when they stood

Where the black crosses hung o'er the Kuttamow flood.

As a derelict ship drifts away with the tide
The Captain went out on the Past from his Bride,

Back, back, through the springs to the chill of the year,
When he hunted the Boh from Maloon to Tsaleer.

As the shape of a corpse dimmers up through deep water,
In his eye lit the passionless passion of slaughter,

And men who had fought with O'Neil for the life
Had gazed on his face with less dread than his wife.

For she who had held him so long could not hold him—
Though a four-month Eternity should have con-trolled him—

But watched the twin Terror—the head turned to head—
The scowling, scarred Black, and the flushed savage Red—

The spirit that changed from her knowing and flew To
Some grim hidden Past she had never a clue to,

But It knew as It grinned, for he touched it un-fearing,
And muttered aloud, 'So you kept that jade ear ring !'

Then nodded, and kindly, as friend nods to friend,
'Old man, you fought well, but you lost in the end.'

The visions departed, and Shame followed Passion,
'He took what I said in this horrible fashion,

'I'll write to Harendra!' With language unsainted

The Captain came back to the Bride . . . who had fainted.

And this is a fiction? No. Go to Simoorie
And look at their baby, a twelve-month old Houri,

A pert little, Irish-eyed Kathleen Mavournin—
She's always about on the Mall of a mornin'—

And you'll see, if her right shoulder-strap is dis-placed,
This: *Gules* upon *argent,* a Boh's Head, *erased!*

THE LAMENT OF THE BORDER CATTLE THIEF

O WOE is me for the merry life
I led beyond the Bar,
And a treble woe for my winsome wife
That weeps at Shalimar.

They have taken away my long jezail,
My shield and sabre fine,
And heaved me into the Central Jail
For lifting of the kine.

The steer may low within the byre,
The Jut may tend his grain,
But there'll be neither loot nor fire
Till I come back again.

And God have mercy on the Jut
When once my fetters fall,
And Heaven defend the farmer's hut
When I am loosed from thrall.

It's woe to bend the stubborn back
Above the grinching quern,
It's woe to hear the leg-bar clack
And jingle when I turn!

But for the sorrow and the shame,
The brand on me and mine,
I'll pay you back in leaping flame
And loss of the butchered kine.

For every cow I spared before
In charity set free,
If I may reach my hold once more
I'll reive an honest three!

For every time I raised the low
That scared the dusty plain,
By sword and cord, by torch and tow
I'll light the land with twain!

Ride hard, ride hard to Abazai,
Young *Sahib* with the yellow hair—
Lie close, lie close as khuttucks lie,
Fat herds below Bonair !

The one I'll shoot at twilight tide,
At dawn I'll drive the other;
The black shall mourn for hoof and hide,
The white man for his brother!

'Tis war, red war, I'll give you then,
War till my sinews fail,
For the wrong you have done to a chief of men

And a thief of the Zukka Kheyl.

And if I fall to your hand afresh
I give you leave for the sin,
That you cram my throat with the foul pig's flesh
And swing me in the skin!

THE RHYME OF THE THREE CAPTAINS

This ballad appears to refer to one of the exploits of the notorious Paul Jones; the American Pirate. It is founded on fact.

… AT the close of a winter day,
Their anchors down, by London town, the Three Great Captains lay.
And one was Admiral of the North from Solway Firth to Skye,
And one was Lord of the Wessex coast and all the lands thereby,
And one was Master of the Thames from Limehouse to Blackwall,
And he was Captain of the Fleet—the bravest of them all.
Their good guns guarded their great grey sides that were thirty foot in the sheer,
When there came a certain trading-brig with news of a privateer.

Her rigging was rough with the clotted drift that drives in a Northern breeze,
Her sides were clogged with the lazy weed that spawns in the Eastern seas.
Light she rode in the rude tide-rip, to left and right she rolled,
And the skipper sat on the scuttle-butt and stared at an empty hold.
'I ha' paid Port dues for your Law quoth he, 'and where is the Law ye boast
'If I sail unscathed from a heathen port to be robbed on a Christian coast?
'Ye have smoked the hives of the Laccadives as we burn the lice in a bunk;
'We tack not now to a Gallang prow or a plunging Pei-ho junk;
'I had no fear but the seas were clear as far as a sail might fare
'Till I met with a lime-washed Yankee brig that rode off Finisterre.
'There were canvas blinds to his bow-gun ports to screen the weight he bore

'And the signals ran for a merchantman from Sandy Hook to the Nore.

'He would not fly the Rovers' flag—the bloody or the black,
'But now he floated the Gridiron and now he flaunted the Jack.
'He spoke of the Law as he crimped my crew—he swore it was only a loan;
'But when I would ask for my own again, he swore it was none of my own.
'He has taken my little parrakeets that nest beneath the Line,
'He has stripped my rails of the shaddock-frails and the green unripened pine;
'He has taken my bale of dammer and spice I won beyond the seas,
' He has taken my grinning heathen gods—and what should he want o' these?
'My foremast would not mend his boom, my deck house patch his boats;
' He has whittled the two this Yank Yahoo, to peddle for shoepeg-oats.
'I could not fight for the failing light and a rough beam-sea beside,
'But I hulled him once for a clumsy crimp and twice because he lied.

'Had I had guns (as I had goods) to work my Christian harm,
'I had run him up from his quarter-deck to trade with his own yard-arm;
'I had nailed his ears to my capstan-head, and ripped them off with a saw,
'And soused them in the bilgewater, and served them to him raw;
'I had flung him blind in a rudderless boat to rot in the rocking dark
'I had towed him aft of his own craft, a bait for his brother shark;
'I had lapped him round with cocoa husk, and drenched him with the oil,
'And lashed him fast to his own mast to blaze above my spoil;
'I had stripped his hide for my hammock-side, and tasselled his beard i' the mesh
'And spitted his crew on the live bamboo that grows through the gangrened flesh;
'I had hove him down by the mangroves brown, where the mud-reef sucks and draws,
'Moored by the heel to his own keel to wait for the land-crab's claws!

He is lazar within and lime without, ye can nose him far enow,
'For he carries the taint of a musky ship—the reek of the slaver's dhow!

' The skipper looked at the tiering guns and the bulwarks tall and cold,
And the Captains Three full courteously peered down at the gutted hole,
And the Captains Three called courteously from deck to scuttle-butt:—
'Good Sir, we ha' dealt with that merchantman or ever your teeth were cut.
'Your words be words of a lawless race, and the Law it standeth thus:
'He comes of a race that have never a Law, and he never has boarded us.
'We ha' sold him canvas and rope and spar—we know that his price is fair,
'And we know that he weeps for the lack of a Law as he rides off Finisterre.
'And since he is damned for a gallows-thief by you and better than you,
'We hold it meet that the English fleet should know that we hold him true.'

The skipper called to the tall taffrail: 'And what is that to me?
'Did ever you hear of a privateer that rifled a Seventy-three ?
'Do I loom so large from your quarter-deck that I lift like a ship o' the Line?
'He has learned to run from a shotted gun and harry such craft as mine.
'There is never a Law on the Cocos Keys to hold a white man in,
'But we do not steal the niggers' meal, for that is a nigger's sin.
'Must he have his Law as a quid to chaw, or laid in brass on his wheel ?
'Does he steal with tears when he buccaneers?
'Fore Gad, then, why does he steal?'
The skipper bit on a deep-sea word, and the word it was not sweet,
For he could see the Captains Three had signalled to the Fleet.
But three and two, in white and blue, the whimpering flags began:
'We have heard a tale of a foreign sail, but he is a merchantman.'

The skipper peered beneath his palm and swore by the Great Horn Spoon,
"Fore Gad, the Chaplain of the Fleet would bless my picaroon!'
By two and three the flags blew free to lash the laughing air,
'We have sold our spars to the merchantman—we know that his price is fair.
' The skipper winked his Western eye, and swore by a China storm: —
'They ha' rigged him a Joseph's jury-coat to keep his honour warm.'
The halliards twanged against the tops, the bunting bellied broad,
The skipper spat in the empty hold and mourned for a wasted cord.

Masthead—masthead, the signal sped by the line o' the British craft;
 The skipper called to his Lascar crew, and put her bout and laughed:—
'It's mainsail haul, my bully boys all—we'll out to the seas again;
'Ere they set us to paint their pirate saint, or scrub at his grapnel-chain

'It's fore-sheet free, with her head to the sea, and the swing of the unbought brine—
'We'll make no sport in an English court till we come as a ship o' the Line,
'Till we come as a ship o' the Line, my lads, of thirty foot in the sheer,
'Lifting again from the outer main with news of a privateer;
'Flying his pluck at our mizzen-truck for weft of Admiralty,
'Heaving his head for our dipsy-lead in sign that we keep the sea.
'Then fore-sheet home as she lifts to the foam—we stand on the outward tack
'We are paid in. the coin of the white man's trade— the bezant is hard, ay, and black.
'The frigate-bird shall carry my word to the Kling and the Orang-Laut
'How a man may sail from a heathen coast to be robbed in a Christian port;
'How a man may be robbed in Christian port while Three Great Captains there
'Shall dip their flag to a slaver's rag—to show that his trade is fair!'

THE BALLAD OF THE 'CLAMPHERDOWN'

IT was our war-ship 'Clampherdown'
Would sweep the Channel clean,
Wherefore she kept her hatches close
When the merry Channel chops arose,
To save the bleached marine.

She had one bow-gun of a hundred ton,
And a great stern-gun beside;
They dipped their noses deep in the sea,
Thy racked their stays and staunchions free
In the wash of the wind-whipped tide.

It was our war-ship 'Clampherdown,
Fell in with a cruiser light
That carried the dainty Hotchkiss gun
And a pair o' heels wherewith to run,
From the grip of a close-fought fight.

She opened fire at seven miles—
As ye shoot at a bobbing cork—
And once she fired and twice she fired,
Till the bow-gun drooped like a lily tired
That lolls upon the stalk.

'Captain, the bow-gun melts apace,
'The deck-beams break below, '
'Twere well to rest for an hour or twain,
'And botch the shattered plates again'
And he answered, 'Make it so.'

She opened fire within the mile—
As ye shoot at the flying duck—
And the great stern-gun shot fair and true,
With the heave of the ship, to the stainless blue,
And the great stern-turret stuck.

'Captain, the turret fills with steam,
'The feed-pipes burst below—
'You can hear the hiss of helpless ram,
'You can hear the twisted runners jam.
And he answered, 'Turn and go!'

It was our war-ship 'Clampherdown,'
And grimly did she roll;

Swung round to take the cruiser's fire
As the White Whale faces the Thresher's ire,
When they war by the frozen Pole.

'Captain, the shells are falling fast,
'And faster still fall we;
'And it is not meet for English stock,
'To bide in the heart of an eight-day clock,
'The death they cannot see.'

'Lie down, lie down my bold A.B.,
'We drift upon her beam;
'We dare not ram for she can run;
'And dare ye fire another gun,
'And die in the peeling steam?'

It was our war-ship 'Clampherdown'
That carried an armour-belt;
But fifty feet at stern and bow,
Lay bare as the paunch of the purser's sow,
To the hail of the Nordenfeldt.

'Captain, they lack us through and through;
'The chilled steel bolts are swift!
'We have emptied the bunkers in open sea,
'Their shrapnel bursts where our coal should be.'
And he answered, ' Let her drift. '

It was our war-ship 'Clampherdown,'
Swung round upon the tide,
Her two dumb guns glared south and north,
And the blood and the bubbling steam ran forth,
And she ground the cruiser's side.

'Captain, they cry, the fight is done,
'They bid you send your sword.'
And he answered, 'Grapple her stern and bow.
'They have asked for the steel. They shall have it now;
'Out cutlasses and board!'

It was our war-ship 'Clampherdown,'
Spewed up four hundred men;
And the scalded stokers yelped delight,
As they rolled in the waist and heard the fight,
Stamp o'er their steel-walled pen.

They cleared the cruiser end to end,
From conning-tower to hold.
They fought as they fought in Nelson's fleet;
They were stripped to the waist, they were bare to the feet,
As it was in the days of old.

It was the sinking 'Clampherdown'
Heaved up her battered side—
And carried a million pounds in steel,
To the cod and the corpse-fed conger-eel,
And the scour of the Channel tide.

It was the crew of the 'Clampherdown'
Stood out to sweep the sea,
On a cruiser won from an ancient foe, As it was in the days of long-ago,
And as it still shall be.

THE BALLAD OF THE 'BOLIVAR'

Seven men from all the world, back to Docks again,

Rolling down the Ratcliffe Road drunk and raising Cain
Give the girls another drink fore we sign away —
We that took the 'Bolivar' out across the Bay!

We put out from Sunderland loaded down with rails;
We put back to Sunderland 'cause our cargo shifted;
We put out from Sunderland—met the winter gales—
Seven days and seven nights to the Start we drifted.

Racketing her rivets loose, smoke-stack white as snow,
All the coals adrift a deck, half the rails below
Leaking like a lobster-pot, steering like a dray—
Out we took the 'Bolivar,' out across the Bay!

One by one the Lights came up, winked and let us by;
Mile by mile we waddled on, coal and fo'c'sle short;
Met a blow that laid us down, heard a bulkhead fly;
Left The Wolf behind us with a two foot-list to port.

Trailing like a wounded duck, working out her soul;
Clanging like a smithy-shop after every roll;
Just a funnel and a mast lurching through the spray—
So we threshed the 'Bolivar' out across the Bay!

Felt her hog and felt her sag, betted when she'd break;
Wondered every time she raced if she'd stand the shock;

THE 'BOLIVAR'

Heard the seas like drunken men pounding at her strake;
Hoped the Lord 'ud keep his thumb on the plummer-block.

Banged against the iron decks, bilges choked with coal;

Flayed and frozen foot and hand, sick of heart and soul;
'Last*we prayed she'd buck herself into Judg-ment Day—
Hi! we cursed the 'Bolivar' knocking round the Bay!

Oh! her nose flung up to sky, groaning to be still—
Up and down and back we went, never time for breath;
Then the money paid at Lloyd's caught her by the heel,
And the stars ran round and round dancin* at our death.
Aching for an hour's sleep, dozing off between;
Heard the rotten rivets draw when she took it green;

Watched the compass chase its tail like a cat at play-
That was on the 'Bolivar,' south across the Bay.

Once we saw between the squalls, lyin' head to swell—
Mad with work and weariness, wishin' they was we—
Some damned Liner's lights go by like a grand hotel;
Cheered her from the 'Bolivar,' swampin' in the sea.

Then a greyback cleared us out, then the skipper laughed;
'Boys, the wheel has gone to Hell—rig the winches aft!
'Yoke the kicking rudder-head—get her under way!'
So we steered her, pulley-haul, out across the Bay!

Just a pack o' rotten plates puttied up with tar,
In we came, an' time enough 'cross Bilbao Bar.

Overloaded, undermanned, meant to founder, We
Euchred God Almighty's storm, bluffed the Eternal Sea!

Seven men from all the world, back to town again,
Rollin' down the Ratcliffe Road drunk and raising Cain :
Seven men from out of HelL Ain't the owners gay,

' Cause we took the 'Bolivar' safe across the Bay ?

THE LOST LEGION

THERE'S a Legion that never was 'listed,
That carries no colours or crest,
But, split in a thousand detachments,
Is breaking the road for the rest.
Our fathers they left us their blessing—
They taught us, and groomed us, and crammed;
But we've shaken the Clubs and the Messes
To go and find out and be damned,
Dear boys!
To go and get shot and be damned.

So some of us chevy the slaver,
And some of us cherish the black,
And some of us hunt on the Oil Coast,
And some on—the Wallaby track:
And some of us drift to Sarawak,
And some of us drift up The Fly,
And some share our tucker with tigers,
And some with the gentle Masai,
Dear boys!
Take tea with the giddy Masai.

We've painted The Islands vermilion,
We' Ve pearled on half-shares in the Bay,
We've shouted on seven-ounce nuggets,
We'Ve starved on a Kanaka's pay.
We've laughed at the world as we found it,—
Its women and cities and men—
From Say Yid Burgash in a tantrum

To the smoke-reddened eyes of Loben, Dear boys !
We've a little account with Loben.

We opened the Chinaman's oil-well,
But the dynamite didn't agree,
And the people got up and fan-kwaied us,
And we ran from Ichang to the sea.
Yes, somehow and somewhere and always
We were first when the trouble began,
From a lottery-row in Manila
To an I. D. B. race on the Pan,
Dear boys!
With the Mounted Police on the Pan.

We preach in advance of the Army,
We skirmish ahead of the Church,
With never a gunboat to help us
When we're scuppered and left in the lurch.
But we know as the cartridges finish
And we're filed on our last little shelves,
That the Legion that never was 'listed
Will send us as good as ourselves,
(Good men!)
Five hundred as good as ourselves.

Then a health (we must drink it in whispers),
To our wholly unauthorised horde—
To the line of our dusty foreloopers,
The Gentlemen Rovers abroad.
Yes, a health to ourselves ere we scatter,
For the steamer won't wait for the train,
And the Legion that never was 'listed
Goes back into quarters again.

'Regards!
Goes back under canvas again.
Hurrah !
The swag and the billy again.
Here's how!
The trail and the packhorse again.
Salue!
The trek and the lager again.

THE SACRIFICE OF ER-HEB

Er-Heb. beyond the Hills of Ao-Safai
Bears witness to the truth, and Ao-Safai
Hath told the men of Gorukh. Thence the tale
Comes westward o'er the peaks to India.

The story of Bisesa, Armod's child,—
A maiden plighted to the Chief in War,
The Man of Sixty Spears who held the Pass
That leads to Thibet, but to-day is gone
To seek his comfort of the God called Budh
The Silent—showing how the Sickness ceased
Because of her who died to save the tribe.

Taman is One and greater than us all,
Taman is One and greater than all Gods:
Taman is Two in One and rides the sky,
Curved like a stallion's croup, from dusk to dawn,
And drums upon it with his heels, whereby
Is bred the neighing thunder in the hills.

This is Taman, the God of all Er-Heb,

Who was before all Gods, and made all Gods,
And presently will break the Gods he made,
And step upon the Earth to govern men
Who give him milk-dry ewes and cheat his
Priests,
Or leave his shrine unlighted—as Er-Heb
Left it unlighted and forgot Taman,
When all the Valley followed after Kysh
And Yabosh, little Gods but very wise,
And from the sky Taman beheld their sin.

He sent the Sickness out upon the hills
The Red Horse Sickness with the iron hooves,
To turn the Valley to Taman again.

And the Red Horse snuffed thrice into the wind,
The naked wind that had no fear of him;
And the Red Horse stamped thrice upon the snow,
The naked snow that had no fear of him;
And the Red Horse went out across the rocks
The ringing rocks that had no fear of him;
And downward, where the lean birch meets the snow

And downward, where the grey pine meets the birch,
And downward, where the dwarf oak meets the pine,
Till at his feet our cup-like pastures lay.

That night, the slow mists of the evening dropped,
Dropped as a cloth upon a dead man's face,
And weltered in the valley, bluish-white
Like water very silent—spread abroad,
Like water very silent, from the Shrine
Unlighted of Taman to where the stream

Is dammed to fill our cattle-troughs—sent up
White waves that rocked and heaved and then were still,
Till all the Valley glittered like a marsh,
Beneath the moonlight, filled with sluggish mist
Knee-deep, so that men waded as they walked.

That night, the Red Horse grazed above the Dam,
Beyond the cattle-troughs. Men heard him feed,
And those that heard him sickened where they lay.

Thus came the sickness to Er-Heb, and slew
Ten men, strong men, and of the women four;
And the Red Horse went hillward with the dawn,
But near the cattle-troughs his hoof-prints lay.

That night, the slow mists of the evening dropped,
Dropped as a cloth upon the dead, but rose
A little higher, to a young girl's height;
Till all the valley glittered like a lake,
Beneath the moonlight, filled with sluggish mist.

That night, the Red Horse grazed beyond the Dam
A stone's throw from the troughs. Men heard him feed,
And those that heard him sickened where they lay.
Thus came the sickness to Er-Heb, and slew
Of men a score, and of the women eight,
And of the children two.

Because the road
To Gorukh was a road of enemies,
And Ao-Safai was blocked with early snow,
We could not flee from out the Valley. Death
Smote at us in a slaughter-pen, and Kysh

Was mute as Yabosh, though the goats were slain;
And the Red Horse grazed nightly by the stream,
And later, outward, towards the Unlighted Shrine,
And those that heard him sickened where they lay.

Then said Bisesa to the Priests at dusk,
When the white mist rose up breast-high and choked
The voices in the houses of the dead:—
'Yabosh and Kysh avail not. If the Horse
'Reach the Unlighted Shrine we surely die.
'Ye have forgotten of all Gods the Chief
'Taman!' Here rolled the thunder through the Hill.
And Yabosh shook upon his pedestal.
'Ye have forgotten of all Gods the chief
'Too long.' And all were dumb save one who cried
On Yabosh with the Sapphire 'twixt His knees
But found no answer in the smoky roof
And, being smitten of the sickness died
Before the altar of the Sapphire Shrine.

Then said Bisesa:—'I am near to Death,
'And have the Wisdom of the Grave for gift
'To bear me on the path my feet must tread.
'If there be wealth on earth, then I am rich,
'For Armod is the first of all Er-Heb;
'If there be beauty on the earth,'—her eyes
Dropped for a moment to the temple floor,—
'Ye know that I am fair. If there be Love,
'Ye know that love is mine.' The Chief in War,

The Man of Sixty Spears, broke from the press,
And would have clasped her, but the Priests with-stood,
Saying:—'She has a message from Tainan.'

Then said Bisesa:—'By my wealth and love
'And beauty, I am chosen of the God
'Tainan.' Here rolled the thunder through the Hills
And Kysh fell forward on the Mound of Skulls.

In darkness and before our Priests, the maid
Between the altars, cast her bracelets down,
Therewith the heavy earrings Armod made,
When he was young, out of the water-gold
Of Gorukh—threw the breast-plate thick with jade
Upon the turquoise anklets—put aside
The bands of silver on her brow and neck;
And as the trinkets tinkled on the stones,
The Thunder of Taman lowed like a bull.

Then said Bisesa stretching out her hands,
As one in darkness fearing Devils:—'Help!
'O Priests, I am a woman very weak.

'And who am I to know the will of Gods?
'Taman hath called me—whither shall I go?'
The Chief in War, the Man of Sixty Spears
Howled in his torment fettered by the Priests
But dared not come to her to drag her forth,
And dared not lift his spear against the Priests.
Then all men wept.

There was a Priest of Kysh
Bent with a hundred winters, hairless, blind
And taloned as the great Snow-Eagle is.
His seat was nearest to the altar-fires,
And he was counted dumb among the Priests.
But, whether Kysh decreed, or from Taman

The impotent tongue found utterance we know
As little as the bats beneath the eaves.
He cried so that they heard who stood without:—
'To the Unlighted Shrine!' and crept aside
Into the shadow of his fallen God
And whimpered, and Bisesa went her way.

That night, the slow mists of the evening dropped,
Dropped as a cloth upon the dead, and rose
Above the roofs, and by the Unlighted Shrine

Lay as the slimy water of the troughs
When murrain thins the cattle of Er-Heb:
And through the mist men heard the Red Horse feed.

In Armod's house they burned Bisesa's dower,
And killed her black bull Tor, and broke her wheel,
And loosed her hair, as for the marriage-feast
With cries more loud than mourning for the dead.

Across the fields, from Armod's dwelling-place,
We heard Bisesa weeping where she passed
To seek the Unlighted Shrine; the Red Horse
Neighed
And followed her, and on the river-mint
His hooves struck dead and heavy in our ears.

Out of the mists of evening, as the star
Of Ao-Safai climbs through the black snow-blur
To show the Pass is clear, Bisesa stepped
Upon the great grey slope of mortised stone,
The Causeway of Taman. The Red Horse neighed
Behind her to the Unlighted Shrine—then fled

North to the Mountain where his stable lies.

They know who dared the anger of Taman,
And watched that night above the clinging mists,
Far up the hill, Bisesa's passing in.

She set her hand upon the carven door,
Fouled by a myriad bats, and black with time,
Whereon is graved the Glory of Taman
In letters older than the Ao-Safai;
And twice she turned aside and twice she wept,
Cast down upon the threshold, clamouring
For him she loved—the Man of Sixty Spears,
And for her father,—and the black bull Tor
Hers and her pride. Yea, twice she turned away
Before the awful darkness of the door,
And the great horror of the Wall of Man
Where Man is made the plaything of Taman,
An Eyeless Face that waits above and laughs.

But the third time she cried and put her palms
Against the hewn stone leaves, and prayed Taman
To spare Er-Heb and take her life for price.

They know who watched, the doors were rent apart
And closed upon Bisesa, and the rain

Broke like a flood across the Valley, washed
The mist away; but louder than the rain
The thunder of Taman filled men with fear.

Some say that from the Unlighted Shrine she cried
For succour, very pitifully, thrice,

And others that she sang and had no fear.
And some that there was neither song nor cry,
But only thunder and the lashing rain.

Howbeit, in the morning, men rose up,
Perplexed with horror, crowding to the Shrine,
And when Er-Heb was gathered at the doors
The Priests made lamentation and passed in
To a strange Temple and a God they feared
But knew not.

From the crevices the grass
Had thrust the altar-slabs apart, the walls
Were grey with stains unclean, the roof-beams
Swelled
With many-coloured growth of rottenness,
And lichen veiled the Image of Taman In leprosy. The Basin of the Blood

Above the altar held the morning sun
A winking ruby on its heart; below,
Face hid in hands, the maid Bisesa lay.

Er-Heb beyond the Hills of Ao-Safai
Bears witness to the truth, and Ao-Safai
Hath told the men of Gorukh. Thence the tale
Comes westward o'er the peaks to India.

THE DOVE OF DACCA

THE freed dove flew to the Rajah's tower—
Fled from the slaughter of Moslem kings—
And the thorns have covered the city of Gaur.

Dove—dove—oh, homing dove !
Little white traitor, with woe on thy wings !

The Rajah of Dacca rode under the wall;
He set in his bosom a dove of flight—
" If she return, be sure that I fall."
Dove—dove—oh, homing dove !
Pressed to his heart in the thick of the fight.

" Fire the palace, the fort, and the keep—
Leave to the foeman no spoil at all.
In the flame of the palace lie down and sleep
If the dove, if the dove—if the homing dove
Come and alone to the palace wall."

The Kings of the North they were scattered abroad—
The Rajah of Dacca he slew them all.
Hot from slaughter he stooped at the ford,
And the dove—the dove—oh, the homing dove !
She thought of her cote on the palace wall.

She opened her wings and she flew away—
Fluttered away beyond recall;
She came to the palace at break of day.
Dove—dove—oh, homing dove !
Flying so fast for a kingdom's fall.

The Queens of Dacca they slept in flame-
Slept in the flame of the palace old—
To save their honour from Moslem shame.
And the dove—the dove—oh, the homing dove !
She cooed to her young where the smoke-cioud rolled.

The Rajah of Dacca rode far and fleet,
Followed as fast as a horse could fly,
He came and the palace was black at his feet;
And the dove—the dove—the homing dove,
Circled alone in the stainless sky.

So the dove flew to the Rajah's tower—
Fled from the slaughter of Moslem kings;
So the thorns covered the city of Gaur,
And Dacca was lost for a white dove's wings.
Dove—dove—oh, homing dove,
Dacca is lost from the roll of the kings !

THE EXPLANATION

LOVE and Death once ceased their strife
At the Tavern of Man's Life.
Called for wine, and threw—alas!—
Each his quiver on the grass.
When the bout was o'er they found
Mingled arrows strewed the ground.
Hastily they gathered then
Each the loves and lives of men.
Ah, the fateful dawn deceived!
Mingled arrows each one sheaved;
Death's dread armoury was stored
With the shafts he most abhorred;
Love's light quiver groaned beneath
Venom-headed darts of Death.

Thus it was they wrought our woe
At the Tavern long ago.
Tell me, do our masters know,

Loosing blindly as they fly,
Old men love while young men die ?

AN ANSWER

A ROSE, in tatters on the garden path,
Cried out to God and murmured 'gainst His wrath,
Because a sudden wind at twilight's hush
Had snapped her stem alone of all the bush.
And God, who hears both sun-dried dust and sun,
Made answer whispering to that luckless one,
" Sister, in that thou sayest We did not well—
What voices heardst thou when thy petals fell?"
And the Rose answered, " In that evil hour
A voice said, 'Father, wherefore falls the flower?
For lo, the very gossamers are still.'
And a voice answered, ' Son, by Allah's will!' "
Then softly as a rain-mist on the sward,
Came to the Rose the Answer of the Lord:
" Sister, before We smote the dark in twain,
Ere yet the stars saw one another plain,
Time, tide, and space, We bound unto the task
That thou shouldst fall, and such an one should ask."
Whereat the withered flower, all content,
Died as they die whose days are innocent;
While he who questioned why the flower fell
Caught hold of God and saved his soul from Hell.

THE GIFT OF THE SEA

THE dead child lay in the shroud,
And the widow watched beside;

And her mother slept, and the Channel swept
The gale in the teeth of the tide.

But the mother laughed at all.
'I have lost my man in the sea,
And the child is dead. Be still,' she said,
'What more can ye do to me?'

The widow watched the dead,
And the candle guttered low,
And she tried to sing the Passing Song
That bids the poor soul go.

And 'Mary take you now,' she sang,
'That lay against my heart.'
And 'Mary smooth your crib to-night,'
But she could not say 'Depart.'

Then came a cry from the sea,
But the sea-rime blinded the glass,
And 'Heard ye nothing, mother?' she said,
"Tis the child that waits to pass.'

And the nodding mother sighed.
"Tis a lambing ewe in the whin,
'For why should the christened soul cry out,
'That never knew of sin? '

'O feet I have held in my hand,
'O hands at my heart to catch,
'How should they know the road to go,
'And how should they lift the latch?'

They laid a sheet to the door,
With the little quilt atop,
That it might not hurt from the cold or the dirt,
But the crying would not stop.

The widow lifted the latch
And strained her eyes to see,
And opened the door on the bitter shore
To let the soul go free.

There was neither glimmer nor ghost,
There was neither spirit nor spark,
And 'Heard ye nothing, mother? ' she said,
"Tis crying for me in the dark.'

And the nodding mother sighed,
"Tis sorrow makes ye dull;
'Have ye yet to learn the cry of the tern,
'Or the wail of the wind-blown gull?'

'The terns are blown inland,
'The grey gull follows the plough.
' 'Twas never a bird, the voice I heard,
'O mother, I hear it now!'

'Lie still, dear lamb, lie still;
'The child is passed from harm,
' 'Tis the ache in your breast that broke your rest,
'And the feel of an empty arm.'

She put her mother aside,
'In Mary's name let be!
'For the peace of my soul I must go,' she said,

And she went to the calling sea.

In the heel of the wind-bit pier,
Where the twisted weed was piled,
She came to the life she had missed by an hour,
For she came to a little child.

She laid it into her breast,
And back to her mother she came,
But it would not feed and it would not heed,
Though she gave it her own child's name.

And the dead child dripped on her breast,
And her own in the shroud lay stark;
And 'God forgive us, mother,' she said,
'We let it die in the dark!

EVARRA AND HIS GODS

Read here,
This is the story of Evarra—man—
Maker of Gods in lands beyond the sea.

Because the city gave him of her gold,
Because the caravans brought turquoises,
Because his life was sheltered by the King,
So that no man should maim him, none should steal,
Or break his rest with babble in the streets
When he was weary after toil, he made
An image of his God in gold and pearl,
With turquoise diadem and human eyes,
A wonder in the sunshine, known afar
And worshipped by the King; but, drunk with pride,

Because the city bowed to him for God,
He wrote above the shrine: ' Thus Gods are made,
'And whoso makes them otherwise shall die?
And all the city praised him. . . . Then he died.

Read here the story of Evarra—man—
Maker of Gods in lands beyond the sea,
Because the city had no wealth to give,
Because the caravans were spoiled afar,
Because his life was threatened by the King,
So that all men despised him in the streets,
He hewed the living rock, with sweat and tears,
And reared a God against the morning-gold,
A terror in the sunshine, seen afar,
And worshipped by the King; but, drunk with pride,
Because the city fawned to bring him back,
He carved upon the plinth: *' Thus Gods are made,*
'And whoso makes them otherwise shall die '
And all the people praised him. . . . Then he died.

Read here the story of Evarra—man—
Maker of Gods in lands beyond the sea.
 Because he lived among a simple folk,
Because his village was between the hills,
Because he smeared his cheeks with blood of ewes,
 He cut an idol from a fallen pine,
Smeared blood upon its cheeks, and wedged a shell

Above its brows for eyes, and gave it hair
Of trailing moss, and plaited straw for crown.
And all the village praised him for this craft,
And brought him butter, honey, milk, and curds.
Wherefore, because the shoutings drove him mad,

He scratched upon that log:' Thus Gods are made,
' And whoso makes them otherwise shall die.'
And all the people praised him. . . Then he died.

Read here the story of Evarra—man—
Maker of Gods in lands beyond the sea,

Because his God decreed one clot of blood
Should swerve one hair's-breadth from the pulse's path,
And chafe his brain, Evarra mowed alone,
Rag-wrapped, among the cattle in the fields,
Counting his fingers, jesting with the trees,
And mocking at the mist, until his God Drove him to labour.
Out of dung and horns
Dropped in the mire he made a monstrous God,
Abhorrent, shapeless, crowned with plaintain tufts,
And when the cattle lowed at twilight time,
He dreamed it was the clamour of lost crowds,

And howled among the beasts: **'Thus Gods are made,**
'And whoso makes them otherwise shall die. '
Thereat the cattle bellowed. . . . Then he died.

Yet at the last he came to Paradise,
And found his own four Gods, and that he wrote;
And marvelled, being very near to God,
What oaf on earth had made his toil God's law,
Till God said mocking: 'Mock not. These be thine.'
Then cried Evarra: 'I have sinned!'—'Not so.
'If thou hadst written otherwise, thy Gods
'Had rested in the mountain and the mine,
'And I were poorer by four wondrous Gods,
'And thy more wondrous law, Evarra. Thine,

'Servant of shouting crowds and lowing kine.'

Thereat, with laughing mouth, but tear-wet eyes,
Evarra cast his Gods from Paradise.

This is the story of Evarra—man—
Maker of Gods in lands beyond the sea.

THE CONUNDRUM OF THE WORKSHOPS

WHEN the flush of a new-born sun fell first on Eden's green and gold,
Our father Adam sat under the Tree and scratched with a stick in the mould;
And the first rude sketch that the world had seen was joy to his mighty heart,
Till the Devil whispered behind the leaves, 'It's pretty, but is it Art?'

Wherefore he called to his wife, and fled to fashion his work anew—
The first of his race who cared a fig for the first, most dread review;
And he left his lore to the use of his sons—and that was a glorious gain
When the Devil chuckled 'Is it Art?' in the ear of the branded Cain.

They builded a tower to shiver the sky and wrench the stars apart,
Till the Devil grunted behind the bricks: 'It's striking, but is it Art? '
The stone was dropped at the quarry-side and the idle derrick swung,
While each man talked of the aims of Art, and each in an alien tongue.

They fought and they talked in the North and the South, they talked and they
fought in the West,
Till the waters rose on the pitiful land, and the poor Red Clay had rest—
Had rest till the dank, blank-canvas dawn when the dove was preened to start,
And the Devil bubbled below the keel: 'It's human, but is it Art? '

The tale is as old as the Eden Tree—and new as the new-cut tooth—
For each man knows ere his lip-thatch grows he is master of Art and Truth;

And each man hears as the twilight nears, to the beat of his dying heart,
The Devil drum on the darkened pane: 'You did it, but was it Art?'

We have learned to whittle the Eden Tree to the shape of a surplice-peg,
We have learned to bottle our parents twain in the yelk of an addled *egg* ,
We know that the tail must wag the dog, for the horse is drawn by the cart;
But the Devil whoops, as he whooped of old: 'It's clever, but is it Art?'

When the flicker of London sun falls faint on the Club-room's green and gold,
The sons of Adam sit them down and scratch with their pens in the mould—
They scratch with their pens in the mould of their graves, and the ink and the anguish start,
For the Devil mutters behind the leaves: 'It's pretty, but is it Art?'

Now, if we could win to the Eden Tree where the Four Great Rivers flow,
And the Wreath of Eve is red on the turf as she left it long ago,
And if we could come when the sentry slept and softly scurry through,
By the favour of God we might know as much— as our father Adam knew.

IN THE NEOLITHIC AGE

IN the Neolithic Age savage warfare did I wage
For food and fame and two-toed horses' pelt;
I was singer to my clan in that dim, red Dawn of Man,
And I sang of all we fought and feared and felt.

Yea, I sang as now I sing, when the Prehistoric spring
Made the piled Biscayan ice-pack split and shove,
And the troll and gnome and dwerg, and the Gods of Cliff and Berg
Were about me and beneath me and above.

But a rival of Solutre* told the tribe my style was *outre*—

By a hammer, grooved of dolomite, he fell.
And I left my views on Art, barbed and tanged, be-neath the heart
Of a mammothistic etcher at Grenelle.

Then I stripped them, scalp from skull, and my hunting dogs fed full,
And their teeth I threaded neatly on a thong;
And I wiped my mouth and said, " It is well that they are dead,
For I know my work is right and theirs was wrong."

But my Totem saw the shame; from his ridgepole shrine he came,
And he told me in a vision of the night: —
" There are nine and sixty ways of constructing tribal lays,
And every single one of them is right!"

Then the silence closed upon me till They put new clothing on me
Of whiter, weaker flesh and bone more frail;
And I stepped beneath Time's finger once again a tribal singer
And a minor poet certified by Tr—1.
Still they skirmish to and fro, men my messmates on the snow,
When we headed off the aurochs turn for turn ;
When the rich Allobrogenses never kept amanuenses,
And our only plots were piled in lakes at Berne.

Still a cultured Christian age sees us scuffle, squeak, and rage,
Still we pinch and slap and jabber—scratch and dirk;
Still we let our business slide—as we dropped the half-dressed hide—
To show a fellow-savage how to work.

Still the world is wondrous large,—seven seas from marge to marge,—
And it holds a vast of various kinds of man ;
And the wildest dreams of Kew are the facts of Khat-mandhu
And the crimes of Clapham chaste in Martaban.

Here's my wisdom for your use, as I learned it when the moose
And the reindeer roared where Paris roars to-night:
There are nine and sixty ways of constructing tribal lays,
And—every—single—one—of—them —is—right.

THE LEGEND OF EVIL

I

THIS is the sorrowful story
Told when the twilight fails
And the monkeys walk together
Holding each other's tails.

'Our fathers lived in the forest,
'Foolish people were they,
'They went down to the cornland
'To teach the farmers to play.

'Our fathers frisked in the millet,
'Our fathers skipped in the wheat,
'Our fathers hung from the branches,
'Our fathers danced in the street.

'Then came the terrible farmers,
'Nothing of play they knew,
'Only . . . they caught our fathers
'And set them to labour too!

'Set them to work in the cornland
'With ploughs and sickles and flails,
'Put them in mud-walled prisons
'And—cut off their beautiful tails!

'Now, we can watch our fathers,
'Sullen and bowed and old,
'Stooping over the millet,
'Sharing the silly mould.

'Driving a foolish furrow,
'Mending a muddy yoke,
'Sleeping in mud-walled prisons,
'Steeping their food in smoke.

'We may not speak to our fathers,
'For if the farmers knew
'They would come up to the forest
'And set us to labour too!'

This is the horrible story
Told as the twilight fails
And the monkeys walk together
Holding each other's tails.

II

'TWAS when the rain fell steady an' the Ark was pitched an' ready,
That Noah got his orders for to take the bastes below;
He dragged them all together by the horn an' hide an' feather,
An' all excipt the Donkey was agreeable to go.

Thin Noah spoke him fairly, thin talked to him severely,
An' thin he cursed him squarely to the glory av the Lord:
'Divil take the ass that bred you, and the greater ass that fed you—
Divil go wid you, ye spalpeen!' an' the Donkey went aboard.

But the wind was always fallin', an' 'twas most onaisy sailin',
An' the ladies in the cabin couldn't stand the stable air;

An' the bastes betwuxt the hatches, they tuk an' died in batches,
Till Noah said: 'There's wan av us that hasn't paid his fare!'

For he heard a flusteration wid the bastes av all creation—
The trumpetin' av elephints an' bellowin' av whales;
An' he saw forninst the windy whin he wint to stop the shindy
The Divil wid a stable-fork bedivillin' their tails.
The Divil cursed outrageous, but Noah said um-brageous :
'To what am I indebted for this tenant-right invasion ?'
An' the Divil gave for answer: 'Evict me if you can, sir,
'For I came in wid the Donkey—on Your Honour's invitation.'

THE ENGLISH FLAG

Above the portico a flag-staff, bearing the Union Jack, remained fluttering in the flames for some time, but ultimately when it fell the crowds rent the air with shouts, and seemed to see significance in the incident.—Daily Papers.

WINDS of the World, give answer? They are whimpering to and fro—
And what should they know of England who only England know?—
The poor little street-bred people that vap6ur and fume and brag,
They are lifting their heads in the stillness to yelp at the English Flag!

Must we borrow a clout from the Boer—to plaster anew with dirt?
An Irish liar's bandage, or an English coward's shirt?
We may not speak of England; her Flag's to sell or share.
What is the Flag of England? Winds of the World, declare!

The North Wind blew:—'From Bergen my steel-shod van-guards go;
'I chase your lazy whalers home from the Disko floe;

'By the great North Lights above me I work the will of God,
' That the liner splits on the ice-field or the Dogger fills with cod.

'I barred my gates with iron, I shuttered my doors with flame,
'Because to force my ramparts your nutshell navies came;
'I took the sun from their presence, I cut them down with my blast,
'And they died, but the Flag of England blew free ere the spirit passed.
'The lean white bear hath seen it in the long, long Arctic night,
'The musk-ox knows the standard that flouts the Northern Light:
'What is the Flag of England? Ye have but my bergs to dare,
'Ye have but my drifts to conquer. Go forth, for it is there!'

The South Wind sighed:—'From The Virgins my mid-sea course was ta'en
'Over a thousand islands lost in an idle main,
'Where the sea-egg flames on the coral and the long-backed breakers croon
'Their endless ocean legends to the lazy, locked lagoon.

'Strayed amid lonely islets, mazed amid outer keys,
'I waked the palms to laughter—I tossed the scud in the breeze—
'Never was isle so little, never was sea so lone,
'But over the scud and the palm-trees an English flag was flown.

'I have wrenched it free from the halliard to hang for a wisp on the Horn;
'I have chased it north to the Lizard—ribboned and rolled and torn;
'I have spread its fold o'er the dying, adrift in a hopeless sea;
'I have hurled it swift on the slaver, and seen the slave set free.

'My basking sunfish know it, and wheeling albatross,
'Where the lone wave fills with fire beneath the
Southern Cross. 'What is the Flag of England? Ye have but my reefs to dare,
'Ye have but my seas to furrow. Go forth, for it is there!'

The East Wind roared:—'From the Kuriles, the Bitter Seas, I come,

'And me men call the Home-Wind, for I bring the English home.
'Look—look well to your shipping! By the breath of my mad typhoon
'I swept your close-packed Praya and beached your best at Kowloon!

'The reeling junks behind me and the racing seas before,
'I raped your richest roadstead—I plundered Singapore!
'I set my hand on the Hoogli; as a hooded snake she rose,
'And I flung your stoutest steamers to roost with the startled crows,

'Never the lotos closes, never the wild-fowl wake,
'But a soul goes out on the East Wind that died for England's sake—
'Man or woman or suckling, mother or bride or maid—
'Because on the bones of the English the English Flag is stayed.

'The desert-dust hath dimmed it, the flying wild-ass knows
'The scared white leopard winds it across the taint-less snows.
'What is the Flag of England? Ye have but my sun to dare,
'Ye have but my sands to travel. Go forth, for it is there!'

The West Wind called:—'In squadrons the thought-less galleons fly
'That bear the wheat and cattle lest street-bred people die.
'They make my might their porter, they make my house their path,
'Till I loose my neck from their rudder and whelm them all in my wrath.

'I draw the gliding fog-bank as a snake is drawn from the hole;
'They bellow one to the other, the frighted ship-bells toll,
'For day is a drifting terror till I raise the shroud with my breath,
'And they see strange bows above them and the two go locked to death.

'But whether in calm or wrack-wreath, whether by dark or day,
'I heave them whole to the conger or rip their plates away,
'First of the scattered legions, under a shrieking sky,
'Dipping between the rollers, the English Flag goes by.

'The dead dumb fog hath wrapped it—the frozen dews have kissed—
'The naked stars have seen it, a fellow-star in the mist.
'What is the Flag of England? Ye have but my breath to dare,
'Ye have but my waves to conquer. Go forth, for it is there!'

'CLEARED'

(IN MEMORY OF A COMMISSION)

HELP for a patriot distressed, a spotless spirit hurt,
Help for an honourable clan sore trampled in the dirt!
From Queenstown Bay to Donegal, O listen to my song,
The honourable gentlemen have suffered grievous wrong.

Their noble names were mentioned— O the burning black disgrace!—
By a brutal Saxon paper in an Irish shooting-case;
They sat upon it for a year, then steeled their heart to brave it,
And 'coruscating innocence' the learned Judges gave it.

Bear witness, Heaven, of that grim crime beneath the surgeon's knife,
The honourable gentleman deplored the loss of life;
Bear witness of those chanting choirs that burk and shirk and snigger,
No man laid hand upon the knife or finger to the trigger!

Cleared in the face of all mankind beneath the winking skies,
Like phoenixes from Phoenix Park (and what lay there) they rise!
Go shout it to the emerald seas—give word to Erin now,
Her honourable gentlemen are cleared—and this is how:—

They only paid the Moonlighter his cattle-hocking price,
They only helped the murderer with council's best advice,

But—sure it keeps their honour white—the learned Court believes
They never gave a piece of plate to murderers and thieves.

They never told the ramping crowd to card a woman's hide,
They never marked a man for death—what fault of theirs he died?—
They only said 'intimidate,' and talked and went away—
By God, the boys that did the work were braver men than they!
Their sin it was that fed the fire—small blame to them that heard—
The 'bhoys' get drunk on rhetoric, and madden at the word—
They knew whom they were talking at, if they were Irish too,
The gentlemen that lied in Court, they knew and well they knew.

They only took the Judas-gold from Fenians out of jail,
They only fawned for dollars on the blood-dyed Clan-na-Gael.
If black is black or white is white, in black and white it's down,
They're only traitors to the Queen and rebels to the Crown.

'Cleared,' honourable gentlemen. Be thankful it's no more:
The widow's curse is on your house, the dead are at your door.
On you the shame of open shame, on you from North to South
The hand of every honest man flat-heeled across your mouth.

'Less black than we were painted'?—Faith, no word of black was said;
The lightest touch was human blood, and that, ye know, runs red.
It's sticking to your fist to-day for all your sneer and scoff,
And by the Judge's well-weighed word you cannot wipe it off.

Hold up those hands of innocence—go, scare your sheep together,
The blundering, tripping tups that bleat behind the old bell-wether;
And if they snuff the taint and break to find another pen,
Tell them it's tar that glistens so, and daub them yours again!

'The charge is old' ?—As old as Cain—as fresh as yesterday;

Old as the Ten Commandments, have ye talked those laws away?
If words are words, or death is death, or powder sends the ball,
You spoke the words that sped the shot—the curse be on you all.

'Our friends believe'?   Of course they do—as sheltered women may;
But have they seen the shrieking soul ripped from the quivering clay?
They!—If their own front door is shut, they'll swear the whole world's
warm;
What do they know of dread of death or hanging fear of harm ?

The secret half a county keeps, the whisper in the lane,
The shriek that tells the shot went home behind the broken pane,
The dry blood crisping in the sun that scares the honest bees,
And shows the 'bhoys' have heard your talk—what do they know of these ?

But you—you know—ay, ten times more; the secrets of the dead,
Black terror on the country-side by word and whisper bred,
The mangled stallion's scream at night, the tail-cropped heifer's low.
Who set the whisper going first? You know, and well you know!

My soul! I'd sooner lie in jail for murder plain and straight,
Pure crime I'd done with my own hand for money, lust, or hate,
Than take a seat in Parliament by fellow-felons cheered,
While one of those 'not provens ' proved me cleared as you are cleared.

Cleared—you that 'lost' the League accounts—go, guard our honour still,
Go, help to make our country's laws that broke God's law at will—
One hand stuck out behind the back, to signal 'strike again ';
The other on your dress-shirt-front to show your heart is clane.

If black is black or white is white, in black and white it's down,
You're only traitors to the Queen and rebels to the Crown.
If print is print or words are words, the learned Court perpends:

We are not ruled by murderers, but only—by their friends.

AN IMPERIAL RESCRIPT

Now this is the tale of the Council the German Kaiser decreed,
To ease the strong of their burden, to help the weak in their need
He sent a word to the peoples, who struggle, and pant, and sweat,
That the straw might be counted fairly and the tally of bricks be set.

The Lords of Their Hands assembled; from the East and the West they drew—
Baltimore, Lille, and Essen, Brummagem, Clyde, and Crewe.
And some were black from the furnace, and some were brown from the soil,
And some were blue from the dye-vat; but all were wearied of toil.

And the young King said 'I have found it, the road to the rest ye seek
'The strong shall wait for the weary, the hale shall halt for the weak;
'With the even tramp of an army where no man breaks from the line,
'Ye shall march to peace and plenty in the bond of brotherhood—sign!'

The paper lay on the table, the strong heads bowed thereby,
And a wail went up from the peoples: 'Ay, sign— give rest, for we die!'
A hand was stretched to the goose-quill, a fist was cramped to scrawl,
When—the laugh of a blue-eyed maiden ran clear through the council-hall.

And each one heard Her laughing as each one saw Her plain—
Saidie, Mimi, or Olga, Gretchen, or Mary Jane.
And the Spirit of Man that is in Him to the light of the vision woke;
And the men drew back from the paper, as a Yankee delegate spoke:—

'There's a girl in Jersey City who works on the telephone;
'We're going to hitch our horses and dig for a house of our own,
'With gas and water connections, and steam-heat through to the top;
' And, W. Hohenzollern,I guess I shall work till I drop.'

And an English delegate thundered: 'The weak an' the lame be blowed!
'I've a berth in. the Sou'-West workshops, a home in the Wandsworth Road;
'And till the 'sociation has footed my bury in' bill, 'I work for the kids an' the missus.
    Pull up! I'll
    be damned if I will!'

And over the German benches the bearded whisper ran:—
' Lager, der girls und der dollars, dey makes or dey breaks a man.
'If Schmitt haf collared der dollars, he collars der girl deremit;
'But if Schmitt bust in der pizness, we collars der girl from Schmitt.'

They passed one resolution: 'Your sub-committee Believe
'You can lighten the curse of Adam when you've lightened the curse of Eve.
'But till we are built like angels—with hammer and chisel and pen,
'We will work for ourself and a woman, for ever and ever. Amen.'

Now this is the tale of the Council the German Kaiser held—
The day that they razored the Grindstone, the day that the Cat was belled,
The day of the Figs from Thistles, the day of the Twisted Sands,
The day that the laugh of a maiden made light of the Lords of Their Hands.

TOMLINSON

Now Tomlinson gave up the ghost in his house in Berkeley Square,
And a Spirit came to his bedside and gripped him by the hair—
A Spirit gripped him by the hair and carried him far away,
Till he heard as the roar of a rain-fed ford the roar of the Milky Way,
Till he heard the roar of the Milky Way die down and drone and cease,
And they came to the Gate within the Wall where Peter holds the keys.
'Stand up, stand up now, Tomlinson, and answer loud and high
'The good that ye did for the sake of men or ever ye came to die—

'The good that ye did for the sake of men in little earth so lone !'

And the naked soul of Tomlinson grew white as a rain-washed bone.
'O, I have a friend on earth,' he said, 'that was my priest and guide,
'And well would he answer all for me if he were by my side.'
—'For that ye strove in neighbour-love it shall be written fair,

'But now ye wait at Heaven's Gate and not in Berkeley Square:
' Though we called your friend from his bed this night, he could not speak for you,
'For the race is run by one and one and never by two and two.
' Then Tomlinson looked up and down, and little gain was there,
For the naked stars grinned overhead, and he saw that his soul was bare:
The Wind that blows between the worlds, it cut him like a knife,
And Tomlinson took up his tale and spoke of his good in life.
'This I have read in a book,' he said, 'and that was told to me,

'And this I have thought that another man thought of a Prince in Muscovy.
' The good souls flocked like homing doves and bade him clear the path,
And Peter twirled the jangling keys in weariness and wrath.
'Ye have read, ye have heard, ye have thought,' he said, 'and the tale is yet to run:
'By the worth of the body that once ye had, give answer—what ha' ye done ?
' Then Tomlinson looked back and forth, and little good it bore,
For the Darkness stayed at his shoulder-blade and Heaven's Gate before:
'Oh, this I have felt, and this I have guessed, and this I have heard men say,
'And this they wrote that another man wrote of a carl in Norroway.'
'Ye have read, ye have felt, ye have guessed, good lack!
Ye have hampered Heaven's Gate;
'There's little room between the stars in idleness to prate!
'Oh, none may reach by hired speech of neighbour, priest, and kin,

'Through borrowed deed to God's good meed that lies so fair within;

'Get hence, get hence to the Lord of Wrong, for doom has yet to run,
'And ... the faith that ye share with Berkeley Square uphold you, Tomlinson! '

The Spirit gripped him by the hair, and sun by sun they fell
Till they came to the belt of Naughty Stars that rim the mouth of Hell:
The first are red with pride and wrath, the next are white with pain,
But the third are black with clinkered sin that cannot burn again:
They may hold their path, they may leave their path, with never a soul to mark,
They may burn or freeze, but they must not cease in the Scorn of the Outer Dark.
The Wind that blows between the worlds, it nipped him to the bone,
And he yearned to the flare of Hell-gate there as the light of his own hearth-stone.

The Devil he sat behind the bars, where the desperate legions drew,

But he caught the hasting Tomlinson and would not let him through.

'Wot ye the price of good pit-coal that I must pay ?' said he,

'That ye rank yoursel' so fit for Hell and ask no leave of me?

'I am all o'er-sib to Adam's breed that ye should give me scorn,

'For I strove with God for your First Father the day that he was born.

'Sit down, sit down upon the slag, and answer loud and high

'The harm that ye did to the Sons of Men or ever you came to die.'

And Tomlinson looked up and up, and saw against the night

The belly of a tortured star blood-red in Hell-Mouth light;

And Tomlinson looked down and down, and saw beneath his feet

The frontlet of a tortured star milk-white in Hell-outh heat.

'Oh, I had a love on earth,' said he, 'that kissed me to my fall,
'And if ye would call my love to me I know she would answer all.'
—'All that ye did in love forbid it shall be written fair,
'But now ye wait at Hell-Mouth Gate and not in Berkeley Square:
'Though we whistled your love from her bed to-night,
I trow she would not run,
'For the sin ye do by two and two ye must pay for one by one!
' The Wind that blows between the worlds, it cut him like a knife,
And Tomlinson took up the tale and spoke of his sin in life:
'Once I ha' laughed at the power of Love and twice at the grip of the Grave,
'And thrice I ha' patted my God on the head that men might call me brave.
' The Devil he blew on a brandered soul and set it aside to cool:
'Do ye think I would waste my good pit-coal on the hide of a brain-sick fool?

'I see no worth in the hobnailed mirth or the jolt-head jest ye did

'That I should waken my gentlemen that are sleep-ing three on a grid.'

Then Tomlinson looked back and forth, and there as little grace,

For Hell-Gate filled the houseless Soul with the
Fear of Naked Space.

'Nay, this I ha' heard,' quo' Tomlinson, 'and this was noised abroad,

'And this I ha' got from a Belgian book on the word
of a dead French lord.'

—'Ye ha' heard, ye ha' read, ye ha' got, good lack!
And the tale begins afresh—

'Have ye sinned one sin for the pride o' the eye or the sinful lust of the flesh?'

Then Tomlinson he gripped the bars and yammered
'Let me in—

'For I mind that I borrowed my neighbour's wife to sin the deadly sin.'

The Devil he grinned behind the bars, and banked the fires high:

'Did ye read of that sin in a book?' said he; and Tomlinson said 'Ay!'

The Devil he blew upon his nails, and the little devils ran;
And he said, 'Go husk this whimpering thief that comes in the guise of a man:
'Winnow him out 'twixt star and star, and sieve his proper worth:
'There's sore decline in Adam's line if this be spawn of earth.
' Empusa's crew, so naked-new they may not face the fire,
But weep that they bin too small to sin to the height of their desire,
Over the coal they chased the Soul, and racked it all abroad,
As children rifle a caddis-case or the raven's foolish hoard.
And back they came with the tattered Thing, as children after play,
And they said: 'The soul that he got from God he has bartered clean away.
'We have threshed a stook of print and book, and winnowed a chattering wind
'

And many a soul wherefrom he stole, but his we cannot find:

'We have handled him, we have dandled him, we have seared him to the bone,
'And sure if tooth and nail show truth he has no soul of his own.
' The Devil he bowed his head on his breast and rumbled deep and low:—
'I'm all o'er-sib to Adam's breed that I should bid him go.

'Yet close we lie, and deep we lie, and if I gave him place,
'My gentlemen that are so proud would flout me to my face;
'They'd call my house a common stews and me a careless host,
'And—I would not anger my gentlemen for the sake of a shiftless ghost.
' The Devil he looked at the mangled Soul that prayed to feel the flame,
And he thought of Holy Charity, but he thought of his own good name:
'Now ye could haste my coal to waste, and sit ye down to fry:
'Did ye think of that theft for yourself?' said he; and Tomlinson said 'Ay!'

The Devil he blew an outward breath, for his heart was free from care:
'Ye have scarce the soul of a louse,' he said, 'but the roots of sin are there,
'And for that sin should ye come in were I the lord alone.
'But sinful pride has rule inside—and mightier than my own.
'Honour and Wit, fore-damned they sit, to each his priest and whore:
'Nay, scarce I dare myself go there, and you they'd torture sore.
'Ye are neither spirit nor spirk,' he said; 'ye are neither book nor brute—
'Go, get ye back to the flesh again for the sake of Man's repute.
'I'm all o'er-sib to Adam's breed that I should mock your pain,
'But look that ye win to worthier sin ere ye come back again.
'Get hence, the hearse is at your door—the grim black stallions wait—
'They bear your clay to place to-day. Speed, lest ye come too late!

'Go back to Earth with a lip unsealed—go back with an open eye,
'And carry my word to the Sons of Men or ever ye come to die:
'That the sin they do by two and two they must pay for one by one—
'And ... the God that you took from a printed book be with you, Tomlinson!'

To T A.

I have made for you a song
 And it may be right or wrong,
But only you can tell me if its true;
I have tried for to explain

Both your pleasure and your pain,
And, Thomas, here's my best respects to you !
Oh, there'll surely come a day
When they'll grant you all your pay,
And treat you as a Christian ought to do ;
So, until that day comes round,
Heaven keep you safe and sound,
And, Thomas, here's my best respects to you.

DANNY DEEVER

'WHAT are the bugles blowin' for?' said Files-on-Parade.
'To turn you out, to turn you out,' the Colour-Sergeant said.
'What makes you look so white, so white?' said Files-on-Parade.
'I'm dreadin' what I've got to watch,' the Colour-Sergeant said.
For they're hangin' Danny Deever, you can hear the Dead March play,
The regiment's in 'ollow square — they're hangin' him to-day;
They've taken of his buttons off an' cut his stripes away,
An' they're hangin' Danny Deever in the mornin'.

'What makes the rear-rank breathe so 'ard?' said Files-on-Parade.
'It's bitter cold, it's bitter cold,' the Colour-Sergeant said.
'What makes that front-rank man fall down?' says . Files-on-Parade.
'A touch o' sun, a touch o' sun,' the Colour-Sergeant said.
They are hangin' Danny Deever, they are marchin' of 'im round,
They 'ave 'alted Danny Deever by 'is coffin on the ground;
An' 'e'll swing in 'arf a minute for a sneakin' shootin' hound—
 O they're hangin' Danny Deever in the mornin'!

' Is cot was right-'and cot to mine,' said Files-on-Parade.
"E's sleepin' out an' far to-night,' the Colour-Sergeant said.
' I've drunk 'is beer a score o' times,' said Files-on-Parade.

' 'E's drinkin' bitter beer alone,' the Colour-Sergeant said.

They are hangin' Danny Deever, you must mark 'im to 'is place,
For 'e shot a comrade sleepin'—you must look 'im in the face;
Nine 'undred of 4s county an' the regiment's disgrace,
While they're hangin1 Danny Deever in the mornin'.

'What's that so black agin the sun?' said Files-on- arade.
'It's Danny fightin' 'ard for life,' the Colour-Sergeant said.
'What's that that whimpers over'ead?' said Files-on-Parade.
'It's Danny's soul that's passin' now,' the Colour-Sergeant said.

For they're done with Danny Deever, you can 'ear the quickstep play,
The regiment's in column, an' they're marchin' us away;
Ho! the young recruits are shakin', an' they'll want their beer to-day,
After hangin'   Danny Deever in   the mornin'.

TOMMY

I WENT into a public-'ouse to get a pint o' beer,
The publican 'e up an' sez, 'We serve no red-coats here.
' The girls be'ind the bar they laughed an' giggled fit to die,
 I outs into the street again an' to myself sez I:

O it's Tommy this, an' Tommy that, an' 'Tommy, go away';
But it's 'Thank you, Mister Atkins,' when the band begins to play,
The band begins to play, my boys, the band begins to play,
O it's 'Thank you, Mister Atkins,' when the band begins to play.

I went into a theatre as sober as could be,
They gave a drunk civilian room, but 'adn't none for me;

They sent me to the gallery or round the music-'alls,

But when it comes to fightin', Lord! they'll shove
me in the stalls!

For it's Tommy this, an' Tommy that, an' 'Tommy, wait outside';
But it's 'Special train for Atkins' when the trooper's on the tide,
The troopship's on the tide, my boys, the troopship's on the tide,
 O it's 'Special train for Atkins' when the trooper's on the tide.

Yes, makin' mock o' uniforms that guard you whileyou sleep
Is cheaper than them uniforms, an' they're starva-tion cheap;

An' hustlin' drunken soldiers when they're goin' large a bit
Is five times better business than paradin' in full kit.

Then it's Tommy this, an' Tommy that, an' 'Tommy, 'ow's yer soul?'
But it's 'Thin red line of 'eroes' when the drums begin to roll,

The drums begin to roll, my boys, the drums begin to roll,
O it's 'Thin red line of 'eroes' when the drums begin to roll.

We aren't no thin red 'eroes, nor we aren't no blackguards too,
But single men in barracks, most remarkable like you;

An' if sometimes our conduck isn't all your fancy paints:
Why, single men in barracks don't grow into plaster saints;

While it's Tommy this, an' Tommy that, an' 'Tommy, fall be'ind,
' But it's'Please to walk in front, sir,' when there's trouble in the wind,
There's trouble in the wind, my boys, there's trouble in the wind,
O it's 'Please to walk in front, sir,' when there's trouble in the wind.

You talk o' better food for us, an' schools, an' fires, an'all:
We'll wait for extry rations if you treat us rational.

Don't mess about the cook-room slops, but prove it to our face
The Widow's Uniform is not the soldier-man's dis-grace.

For it's Tommy this, an' Tommy that, an' 'Chuck him out, the brute!
' But it's 'Saviour of 'is country,' when the guns begin to shoot;
Yes it's Tommy this, an' Tommy that, an' anything you please;
But Tommy ain't a bloomin' fool—you bet hat Tommy sees!

'FUZZY-WUZZY'

(SOUDAN EXPEDITIONARY FORCE)

WE'VE fought with many men acrost the seas,
An' some of 'em was brave an' some was not
The Paythan an' the Zulu an' Burmese;
But the Fuzzy was the finest o' the lot
We never got a ha'porth's change of 'im:
'E squatted in the scrub an' 'ocked our 'orses,
'E cut our sentries up at Suakim,
An' 'e played the cat an' banjo with our forces.

So 'ere's *to* you, Fuzzy-Wuzzy, at your 'ome in the Soudan;
You're a pore benighted 'eathen but a first-class fightin' man;
We gives you your certificate, an' if you want it signed
We'll come an' 'ave a romp with you when-ever you're inclined.

We took our chanst among the Kyber 'ills,
The Boers knocked us silly at a mile,
The Burman give us Irriwaddy chills,
An' a Zulu impi dished us up in style:
But all we ever got from such as they
Was pop to what the Fuzzy made us swaller;

We 'eld our bloomin' own, the papers say,
But man for man the Fuzzy knocked us 'oiler.
Then 'ere's to you, Fuzzy-Wuzzy, an' the missis and the kid;
Our orders was to break you, an' of course we went an' did.
We sloshed you with Martinis, an' it wasn't 'ardly fair;
But for all the odds agin' you, Fuzzy-Wuz you broke the square.

'E 'asn't got no papers of 'is own,
'E 'asn't got no medals nor rewards,
So we must certify the skill 'e's shown
In usin' of 'is long two-'anded swords:
When 'e's 'oppin' in an' out among the bush
With 'is coffin-'eaded shield an' shovel-spear,
An 'appy day with Fuzzy on the rush
Will last an 'ealthy Tommy for a year.

So 'ere's to you, Fuzzy-Wuzzy, an' your friends which are no more,
If we 'adn't lost some messmates we would 'elp you to deplore;
But give an' take's the gospel, an' we'll call the bargain fair,
For if you 'ave lost more than us, you crumpled up the square!

'E rushes at the smoke when we let drive,
An', before we know, 'e's 'ackin' at our 'ead;
'E's all 'ot sand an' ginger when alive,
An' e's generally shammin' when 'e's dead.
'E's a daisy, 'e's a ducky, 'e's a lamb!
'E's a injia-rubber idiot on the spree,
'E's the on'y thing that doesn't give a damn
For a Regiment o' British Infantree!
So 'ere's to you, Fuzzy-Wuzzy, at your 'ome in the Soudan;
You're a pore benighted 'eathen but a first-class fightin' man;
An' 'ere's to you, Fuzzy-Wuzzy, with your 'ayrick 'ead of 'air—
You big black boundin' beggar—for you broke a British square!

SOLDIER, SOLDIER

'SOLDIER, soldier, come from the wars,
Why don't you march with my true love ?'
'We're fresh from off the ship an' 'e's maybe give the slip,
An' you'd best go look for a new love.'

New love! True love!
Best go look for a new love,
The dead they cannot rise, an' you'd better dry your eyes,
An' you'd best go look for a new love.

'Soldier, soldier, come from the wars,
What did you see o' my true love?'
'I seed 'im serve the Queen in a suit o' rifle-green,
An' you'd best go look for a new love.'

'Soldier, soldier, come from the wars,
Did ve see no more o' my true love ?'
'I seed 'im runnin' by when the shots begun to fly—
But you'd best go look for a new love.'

'Soldier, soldier, come from the wars,
Did aught take 'arm to my true love?'
'I couldn't see the fight, for the smoke it lay so white—
An' you'd best go look for a new love.'

'Soldier, soldier, come from the wars,
I'll up an' tend to my true love!'
"E's lying on the dead with a bullet through 'is 'ead,
An' you'd best go look for a new love.'

'Soldier, soldier, come from the wars,
I'll down an' die with my true love!'
'The pit we dug'll 'ide 'im an' the twenty men beside 'im—
An' you'd best go look for a new love.'

'Soldier, soldier, come from the wars,
Do you bring no sign from my true love?'
'I bring a lock of 'air that 'e alius used to wear,
An' you'd best go look for a new love.'

'Soldier, soldier, come from the wars,
O then I know it's true I've lost my true love!'
'An' I tell you truth again—when you've lost the feel o' pain
You'd best take me for your true love.'

True love! New love!
Best take 'im for a new love.
The dead they cannot rise, an' you'd better dry your eyes,
An' you'd best take 'im for your true love.

SCREW-GUNS

SMOKIN' my pipe on the mountings, sniffin' the mornin' cool,
I walks in my old brown gaiters along o' my old brown mule,
With seventy gunners be'ind me, an' never a beggar Forgets
It's only the pick of the Army that handles the dear little pets—'Tss! 'Tss!

For you all love the screw-guns, the screw-guns they all love you!
So when we call round with a few guns, o?
course you will know what to do—hoo! hoo!
Jest send in your Chief an' surrender—it's worse if you fights or you runs:

You can go where you please, you can skid up the trees, but you don't get away from the guns.

They sends us along where the roads are, but mostly we goes where they ain't:
We'd climb up the side of a sign-board an' trust to the stick o' the paint:
We've chivied the Naga an' Looshai, we've give the Afreedeeman fits,
For we fancies ourselves at two thousand, we guns that are built in two bits—
'Tss! 'Tss!
For you all love the screw-guns, etc.

If a man doesn't work, why, we drills 'im an' teaches 'im 'ow to behave;
If a beggar can't march, why, we kills 'im an' rattles 'im into 'is grave.
You've got to stand up to our business an' spring without snatchin' or fuss.
D'you say that you sweat with the field-guns? By God, you must lather with us—'Tss! 'Tss!
For you all love the screw-guns, etc.

The eagles is screamin' around us, the river's a- moanin' below,
We're clear o' the pine an' the oak-scrub, we're out on the rocks an' the snow,

An' the wind is as thin as a whip-lash what carries away to the plains
The rattle an' stamp o' the lead-mules—the jinglety- jink o' the chains—'Tss! 'Tss!
For you all love the screw-guns, etc.

There's a wheel on the Horns o' the Mornin', an' a wheel on the edge o' the Pit,
An' a drop into nothin' beneath you as straight as a beggar can spit:
With the sweat runnin' out o' your shirt-sleeves, an' the sun off the snow in your face,
An' 'arf o' the men on the drag-ropes to hold the old gun in 'er place—'Tss! 'Tss!
For you all love the screw-guns, etc'

Smokin' my pipe on the mountings, sniffin' the mornin' cool,
I climbs in my old brown gaiters along o' my old brown mule.

The monkey can say what our road was—the wild-goat 'e knows where we
passed.

Stand easy, you long-eared old darlin's! Out drag-ropes! With shrapnel! Hold
fast—'Tss! 'Tss!

For you all love the screw-guns—the screw-guns they all love you!
So when we take tea with a few guns, o'
course you will know what to do—hoo! hoo!
Just send in your Chief and surrender—it's
worse if you fights or you runs:

You may hide in the caves, they'll be only
your graves, but you can't get away from the guns!

CELLS

I'VE a head like a concertina: I've a tongue like a button-stick:
I've a mouth like an old potato, and I'm more than a little sick,
But I've had my fun o' the Corp'ral's Guard: I've made the cinders fly,
And I'm here in the Clink for a thundering drink and blacking the Corporal's
eye.

With a second-hand overcoat under my head,
And a beautiful view of the yard,
Oh, it's pack-drill for me and a fortnight's C.B.
For 'drunk and resisting the Guard!'
Mad drunk and resisting the Guard—
'Strewth, but I socked it them hard!
So it's pack-drill for me and a fortnight's C.B,
For 'drunk and resisting the Guard.'

I started o' canteen porter, I finished o' canteen beer,
But a dose o' gin that a mate slipped in, it was that brought me here.

'Twas that and an extry double Guard that rubbed my nose in the dirt;
But I fell away with the Corp'ral's stock and the best of the Corp'ral's shirt.

I left my cap in a public-house, my boots in the public road,
And Lord knows where, and I don't care, my belt and my tunic goed,
They'll stop my pay, they'll cut away the stripes I used to wear,
But I left my mark on the Corp'ral's face, and I think he'll keep it there!

My wife she cries on the barrack-gate, my kid in the barrack-yard,
It ain't that I mind the Ord'ly room—it's ***that*** that cuts so hard.
I'll take my oath before them both that I will sure abstain,
But as soon as I'm in with a mate and gin, I know I'll do it again!

With a second-hand overcoat under my head
And a beautiful view of the yard,
Yes, it's pack-drill for me and a fortnight's C.B.
For 'drunk and resisting the Guard.'
Mad drunk and resisting the Guard—
'Strewth, but I socked it them hard!
So it's pack-drill with me and a fortnight's C.B.
For 'drunk and resisting the Guard.'

GUNGA DIN

You may talk o' gin and beer
When you're quartered safe out 'ere,
An' you're sent to penny-fights an' Aldershot it;
But when it comes to slaughter
You will do your work on water,
An' you'll lick the bloomin' boots of 'im that's got it,
Now in Injia's sunny clime,
Where I used to spend my time
A-servin' of 'Er Majesty the Queen,

Of all them blackfaced crew
The finest man I knew
Was our regimental bhisti, Gunga Din,

He was'Din! Din! Din!
You limping lump o' brick-dust, Gunga Din!
Hi! slippery hitherao!
Water, get it! Panee lao![2]
You squidgy-nosed old idol, Gunga Din.'
The uniform 'e wore Was nothin' much before,

    [2] Bring water swiftly.

An' rather less than 'arf o' that be'ind,
For a piece o' twisty rag
An' a goatskin water-bag
Was all the field-equipment 'e could find.
When the sweatin' troop-train lay
In a sidin' through the day,
Where the 'eat would make your bloomin' eyebrows crawl,
We shouted 'Harry By!'[3]
Till our throats were bricky-dry,
Then we wopped 'im 'cause 'e couldn't serve us all.
It was'Din! Din! Din!
You 'eathen, where the mischief 'ave you been?
You put some juldee[4] in it
Or I'll marrow you this minute[5]
If you don't fill up my helmet, Gunga Din!

'E would dot an' carry one
Till the longest day was done;
An' 'e didn't seem to know the use o' fear.
If we charged or broke or cut,

You could bet your bloomin' nut,
'E'd be waitin' fifty paces right flank rear.

[3] Mr. Atkins' equivalent for ' O brother.'

[4]Be quick.

[5] Hit you.

With 'is mussick1 on 'is back,
'E would skip with our attack,
An' watch us till the bugles made '
Retire,' An' for all 'is dirty 'ide
'E was white, clear white, inside
When 'e went to tend the wounded under fire!
It was'Din! Din! Din!'
With the bullets kickin' dust-spots on the green.
When the cartridges ran out,
You could hear the front-files shout,
'Hi! ammunition-mules an' Gunga Din!'

I sha'n't forgit the night
When I dropped be'ind the fight
With a bullet where my belt-plate should 'a' been.
I was choking' mad with thirst,
An' the man that spied me first
Was our good old grinning gruntin* Gunga Din.
'E lifted up my 'ead,
An' he plugged me where I bled,
An' 'e guv me 'arf-a-pint o' water-green:
It was crawlin' and it stunk,
But of all the drinks I've drunk,
I'm gratefullest to one from Gunga Din.

It was'Din! Din! Din!'
'Ere's a beggar with a bullet through 'is spleen;
'E's chawin' up the ground,
An' 'e's kickin' all around:
For Gawd's sake git the water, Gunga Din!

'E carried me away
To where a dooli lay,
An' a bullet come an' drilled the beggar clean.
'E put me safe inside, An' just before 'e died:
'I 'ope you liked your drink,' sez Gunga Din.
So I'll meet 'im later on
At the place where 'e is gone—
Where it's always double drill and no canteen;
'E'll be squattin' on the coals,
Givin' drink to poor damned souls,
An' I'll get a swig in hell from Gunga Din!
Yes, Din! Din! Din!
You Lazarushian-leather Gunga Din!
Though I've belted you and flayed you,
By the living Gawd that made you,
You're a better man than I am, Gunga Din!

OONTS

(NORTHERN INDIA TRANSPORT TRAIN)

WOT makes the soldier's 'eart to penk, wot makes
him to perspire?
It isn't standin' up to charge nor lyin' down to fire;
But it's everlastin' waitin' on a everlastin' road
For the commissariat camel an' 'is commissariat load.

O the oont,[6] O the oont, O the commissariat oont!
With 'is silly neck a-bobbin' like a basket full o' snakes;
We packs 'im like an idol, an' you ought to 'ear 'im grunt,
An' when we gets 'im loaded up 'is blessed girth-rope breaks.

Wot makes the rear-guard swear so 'ard when night
is drorin' in,
An' every native follower is shiverin' for 'is skin?

[6] Camel—oo is pronounced like u in ' bull,' but by Mr. Atkins to
rhyme with' front.'

It ain't the chanst o' being rushed by Paythans from the 'ills,
It's the commissariat camel puttin' on 'is bloomin' frills!
O the oont, O the oont, O the hairy scary oont!
A-trippin' over tent-ropes when we've got the night alarm!
We socks 'im with a stretcher-pole an' 'eads 'im off in front,
An' when we've saved 'is bloomin' life 'e chaws our bloomin' arm.

The 'orse 'e knows above a bit, the bullock's but a fool,
The elephant's a gentleman, the battery-mule's a mule;
But the commissariat cam-u-el, when all is said an' done,
'E 's a devil an' a ostrich an' a orphan-child in one.
O the oont, O the oont, O the Gawd-forsaken oont!
The lumpy-'umpy 'ummin'-bird a-singin' where 'e lies,

'E's blocked the whole division from the rear-guard to the front,
An' when we get him up again—the beggar goes an' dies!

'E'll gall an' chafe an' lame an' fight—'e smells most awful vile;
'E'll lose isself for ever if you let Mm stray a mile;
'E's game to graze the 'ole day long an' 'owl the 'ole night through,

An' when 'e comes to greasy ground 'e splits isself in two.
O the oont, O the oont, O the floppin', droppin' oont!
When Ms long legs give from under an' is meltin' eye is dim,
The tribes is up be'ind us, and the tribes is out in front—
It ain't no jam for Tommy, but it's kites an' crows for im.

So when the cruel march is done, an' when the roads is blind,
An' when we sees the camp in front an' 'ears the shots be'ind,

Ho then we strips 'is saddle off, and all 'is woes is past:
'E thinks on us that used 'im so, and gets revenge at last.
O the oont, O the oont, O the floatin', bloatin' oont!
The late lamented camel in the water-cut 'e lies;
We keeps a mile behind 'im an' we keeps a mile in front,
But 'e gets into the drinkin'-casks, and then o' course we dies.

LOOT

IF you've ever stole a pheasant-egg be'ind the keeper's back,
If you've ever snigged the washin' from the line,
If you've ever crammed a gander in your bloomin' 'aversack,
You will understand this little song o' mine.
But the service rules are 'ard, and from such we are debarred,
For the same with English morals does not suit.
(*Cornet* : Toot! toot!)
W'y, they call a man a robber if 'e stuffs 'is marchin' clobber
With the—
(*Chorus*) Loo! loo! Lulu! lulu! Loo! loo! Loot! loot! loot!
Ow the loot!
Bloomin' loot!
That's the thing to make the boys git up an'
shoot!

It's the same with dogs an' men,
If you'd make 'em come again
Clap 'em forward with a Loo! loo! Lulu! Loot!
(*ff*) Whoopee! Tear 'im, puppy! Loo! loo! Lulu!
Loot! loot! loot!

If you've knocked a nigger edgeways when e's
thrustin' for your life,
You must leave 'im very careful where 'e fell;
An' may thank your stars an' gaiters if you didn't
feel 'is knife
That you ain't told off to bury 'im as well.
Then the sweatin' Tommies wonder as they spade
the beggars under
Why lootin' should be entered as a crime;
So if my song you'll 'ear, I will learn you plain an'
clear
'Ow to pay yourself for fightin' overtime (*Chorus.*) With the loot, etc.
Now remember when you're 'acking round a gilded Burma god
That 'is eyes is very often precious stones;

An' if you treat a nigger to a dose o' cleanin'-rod
'E's like to show you everything 'e owns.
When 'e won't prodooce no more, pour some water on the floor
Where you 'ear it answer 'ollow to the boot
(*Cornet* : Toot! toot!)—
When the ground begins to sink, shove your baynick down the chink,
An' you're sure to touch the—
(*Chorus.*) Loo! loo! Lulu! Loot! loot! loot!
Ow the loot! etc.

When from 'ouse to 'ouse you're 'unting, you must always work in pairs—
It 'alves the gain, but safer you will find—

For a single man gets bottled on them twisty-wisty stairs,
An' a woman comes and clobs 'im from be'ind.
When you've turned 'em inside out, an' it seems beyond a doubt
As if there weren't enough to dust a flute
(**Comet** : Toot! toot!)—

Before you sling your 'ook, at the 'ouse-tops take a look,
For it's underneath the tiles they 'ide the loot.
(**Chorus** .) Ow the loot, etc.

You can mostly square a Sergint an' a Quartermaster too,
If you only take the proper way to go;
I could never keep my pickin's, but I've learned you all I knew—
An' don't you never say I told you so.
An' now I'll bid good-by, for Pra gettin' rather dry,
An' I see another tunin' up to toot (**Cornet** : Toot! toot!)—
So 'ere's good-luck to those that wears the Widow's clo'es,
 An' the Devil send 'em all they want o' loot!
(**Chorus** .) Yes, the loot,
Bloomin' loot.
In the tunic an' the mess-tin an' the boot!
It's the same with dogs an' men,
If you'd make 'em come again
(*fff*) Whoop 'em forward with a Loo! loo! Lulu! Loot! loot! loot!
Heeya! Sick 'im, puppy! Loo! loo! Lulu! Loot! loot! loot!

'SNARLEYOW

THIS 'appened in a battle to a batt'ry of the corps
Which is first among the women an' amazin' first in war;
An' what the bloomin' battle was I don't remember now,
But Two's off-lead 'e answered to the name o' **Snark Yow** .

Down in the Infantry, nobody cares;
Down in the Cavalry, Colonel 'e swears;
But down in the lead with the wheel at the flog
Turns the bold Bombardier to a little whipped dog!

They was movin' into action, they was needed very sore,
To learn a little schoolin' to a native army corps,

They 'ad nipped against an uphill, they was tuckin' down the brow,
When a tricky, trundlin' round-shot give the knock to ***Snarleyow*** .

They cut 'im loose an' left 'im—'e was almost tore in two—
But he tried to follow after as a well-trained 'orse should do;
'E went an' fouled the limber, an' the Driver's Brother squeals:
'Pull up, pull up for Snarleyaw—'is 'ead's between 'is 'eels!'

The Driver 'umped 'is shoulder, for the wheels was goin' round,
An' there aren't no 'Stop, conductor!' when a batt'ry's changin' ground;
Sez 'e: 'I broke the beggar in, an' very sad I feels,
But I couldn't pull up, not for you—your 'ead be-tween your 'eels!'

'E 'adn't 'ardly spoke the word, before a droppin' Shell
A little right the batt'ry an' between the sections fell;
An' when the smoke 'ad cleared away, before the limber wheels,
There lay the Driver's Brother with 'is 'ead between 'is 'eels.

Then sez the Driver's Brother, an' 'is words was very plain,
'For Gawd's own sake get over me, an' put me out o' pain.'
They saw 'is wounds was mortial, an' they judged that it was best,
So they took an' drove the limber straight across 'is back an' chest.

The Driver 'e give nothin' 'cept a little coughin' grunt,

But 'e swung 'is 'orses 'andsome when it came to 'Action front!'
An' if one wheel was juicy, you may lay your Mon-day head
'Twas juicier for the niggers when the case begun to spread.

The moril of this story, it is plainly to be seen:
You 'avn't got no families when servin' of the Queen—
You 'avn't got no brothers, fathers, sisters, wives, or sons—
If you want to win your battles take an' work your bloomin' guns!

Down in the Infantry, nobody cares;
Down in the Cavalry, Colonel 'e swears;
But down in the lead with the wheel at the flog
Turns the bold Bombardier to a little whipped dog!

THE WIDOW AT WINDSOR

'AVE you 'eard o' the Widow at Windsor
With a hairy gold crown on 'er 'ead?
She 'as ships on the foam—she 'as millions at 'ome,
An' she pays us poor beggars in red.
(Ow, poor beggars in red!)
There's 'er nick on the cavalry 'orses,
There's 'er mark on the medical stores—
An' 'er troopers you'll find with a fair wind be'ind
That takes us to various wars.
(Poor beggars!—barbarious wars!)

Then 'ere's to the Widow at Windsor,
An' 'ere's to the stores an' the guns,
The men an' the 'orses what makes up the Forces
O' Missis Victorier's sons. (Poor beggars ! Victorier's sons!)

Walk wide o' the Widow at Windsor,

For 'alf o' Creation she owns:
We 'ave bought 'er the same with the sword an' the flame,
An' we've salted it down with our bones.
(Poor beggars!—it's blue with our bones!)
Hands off o' the sons of the Widow,
Hands off o' the goods in 'er shop,
For the Kings must come down an' the Emperors Frown
When the Widow at Windsor says 'Stop'!
(Poor beggars!—we're sent to say 'Stop'!)

Then 'ere's to the Lodge o' the Widow,
From the Pole to the Tropics it runs—
To the Lodge that we tile with the rank an' the file,
An' open in form with the guns.
(Poor beggars!—it's always they guns!)

We 'ave 'eard o' the Widow at Windsor,
It's safest to leave 'er alone :
For 'er sentries we stand by the sea an' the land
Wherever the bugles are blown.
(Poor beggars!—an' don't we get blown!)

Take 'old o' the Wings o' the Mornin',
An' flop round the earth till you're dead;
But you won't get away from the tune that they play
To the bloomin' old Rag over'ead.
(Poor beggars!—it's 'ot over'ead!)

Then 'ere's to the sons o' the Widow
Wherever, 'owever they roam.
'Ere's all they desire, an' if they require
A speedy return to their 'ome.
(Poor beggars!—they'll never see ome!)

BELTS

THERE was a row in Silver Street that's near to Dublin Quay,
Between an Irish regiment an' English cavalree;
It started at Revelly an' it lasted on till dark:
The first man dropped at Harrison's, the last forninst the Park.

For it was 'Belts, belts, belts, an' that's one for you!'
An' it was 'Belts, belts, belts, an' that's done for you!'
O buckle an' tongue
Was the song that we sung
From Harrison's down to the Park!

There was a row in Silver Street—the regiments was out,
They called us 'Delhi Rebels,' an' we answered 'Threes about!'
That drew them like a hornet's nest—we met them good an' large,
The English at the double an' the Irish at the charge.
Then it was: Belts—

There was a row in Silver Street—an' I was in it too;
We passed the time o' day, an' then the belts went whirraru!
I misremember what occurred, but subsequint the Storm
A ***Freeman's Journal Supplemint was*** all my uniform.
O it was: Belts—

There was a row in Silver Street—they sent the Polis there,
The English were too drunk to know, the Irish didn't care;
But when they grew impertinint we simultaneous rose,
Till half o' them was Liffey mud an' half was tatthered clo'es.
For it was: Belts—

There was a row in Silver Street—it might ha raged till now,

But some one drew his side-arm clear, an' nobody knew how;
'Twas Hogan took the point an' dropped; we saw the red blood run:
An' so we all was murderers that started out in fun.
While it was: Belts—

There was a row in Silver Street—but that put down the shine,
Wid each man whisperin' to his next: "'Twas never work o' mine!'
We went away like beaten dogs, an' down the street we bore him,
The poor dumb corpse that couldn't tell the bhoys were sorry for him.
When it was: Belts—

There was a row in Silver Street—it isn't over yet,
For half of us are under guard wid punishments to get;

'Tis all a merricle to me as in the Clink I lie:
There was a row in Silver Street—begod, I wonder why!
But it was 'Belts, belts, belts, an' that's one for you!'
An' it was 'Belts, belts, belts, an' that's done for you!'
O buckle and tongue
Was the song that we sung
From Harrison's down to the Park!

THE YOUNG BRITISH SOLDIER

WHEN the 'arf-made recruity goes out to the East
'E acts like a babe an' 'e drinks like a beast,
An' 'e wonders because 'e is frequent deceased
Ere 'e's fit for to serve as a soldier,
Serve, serve, serve as a soldier,
Serve, serve, serve as a soldier,
Serve, serve, serve as a soldier,
So-oldier of the Queen!

Now all you recruities what's drafted to-day,
 You shut up your rag-box an' 'ark to my lay,
An' I'll sing you a soldier as far as I may:
A soldier what's fit for a soldier.
Fit, fit, fit for a soldier.

First mind you steer clear o' the grog-sellers' huts,
For they sell you Fixed Bay'nets that rots out your guts-
Ay, drink that 'ud eat the live steel from your butts—
An' it's bad for the young British soldier.
Bad, bad, bad for the soldier.

When the cholera comes—as it will past a doubt—
Keep out of the wet and don't go on the shout,
For the sickness gets in as the liquor dies out,
An' it crumples the young British soldier.
Crum-, crum-, crumples the soldier. . .

But the worst o' your foes is the sun over'ead:
You *must* wear your 'elmet for all that is said:
If 'e finds you uncovered 'e'll knock you down dead,
An' you'll die like a fool of a soldier.
Fool, fool, fool of a soldier. . .

If you're cast for fatigue by a sergeant unkind,
Don't grouse like a woman nor crack on nor blind;
Be handy and civil and then you will find
That it's beer for the young British soldier.
Beer, beer, beer for the soldier. . .

Now, if you must marry, take care she is old—
A troop-sergeant's widow's the nicest I'm told—
For beauty won't help if your rations is cold,

Nor love ain't enough for a soldier.
'Nough, 'nough, 'nough for a soldier. .

If the wife should go wrong with a comrade, be loth
To shoot when you catch 'em—you'll swing, on my oath !—
Make 'im take 'er and keep 'er: that's Hell for them both,
An' you're shut o' the curse of a soldier.
Curse, curse, curse o' a soldier. . .

When first under fire an' you're wishful to duck,
Don't look nor take 'eed at the man that is struck,
Be thankful you're livin', and trust to your luck
And march to your front like a soldier.
Front, front, front like a soldier. . .

When 'arf of your bullets fly wide in the ditch,
Don't call your Martini a cross-eyed old'bitch;
She's human as you are—you treat her as sich,
An' she'll fight for the young British soldier.
Fight, fight, fight for the soldier. . .

When shakin' their bustles like ladies so fine,
The guns o' the enemy wheel into line;
Shoot low at the limbers an' don't mind the shine,
For noise never startles the soldier.
Start-, start-, startles the soldier. . .

If your officer's dead and the sergeants look white,
Remember it's ruin to run from a fight:
So take open order, lie down, and sit tight,
And wait for supports like a soldier.
Wait, wait, wait like a soldier. . .

When you're wounded and left on Afghanistan's plains,
And the women come out to cut up what remains,
Jest roll to your rifle and blow out your brains
An' go to your Gawd like a soldier.
Go, go, go like a soldier,
Go, go, go like a soldier,
Go, go, go like a soldier,
So-oldier of the Queen!

MANDALAY

BY the old Moulmein Pagoda, lookin' eastward to the sea,
There's a Burma girl a-settin', and I know she thinks o' me;
For the wind is in the palm-trees, and the temple-bells they say:
'Come you back, you British soldier; come you back to Mandalay!'

Come you back to Mandalay,
Where the old Flotilla lay:
Can't you 'ear their paddles chunkin from
Rangoon to Mandalay?
On the road to Mandalay,
Where the fly in'-fishes play,
An' the dawn comes up like thunder outer
China 'crost the Bay!

'Er petticoat was yaller an' 'er little cap was green,
An' 'er name was Supi-yaw-lat—jes' the same as Theebaw's Queen,
An' I seed her first a-smokin' of a whackin' white cheroot,
An' a-wastin' Christian kisses on an 'eathen idol's foot:

Bloomin' idol made o' mud—
What they called the Great Gawd Budd—
Plucky lot she cared for idols when I kissed

'er where she stud!
On the road to Mandalay, etc.

When the mist was on the rice-fields an' the sun was droppin' slow,
She'd git 'er little banjo an' she'd sing l***Kulla-lo-lo'***
With 'er arm upon my shoulder an' 'er cheek agin my cheek
We useter watch the steamers an' the ***hathis*** pilin' teak.
Elephints a-pilin' teak
In the sludgy, squdgy creek,
Where the silence 'ung that 'eavy you was
'arf afraid to speak!
On the road to Mandalay, etc.

But that's all shove be'ind me—long ago an' fur away,
An' there ain't no 'busses runnin' from the Bank to Mandalay;
An' I'm learnin' 'ere in London what the ten-year soldier tells:
'If you've 'eard the East a-callin', you won't never 'eed naught else.'

No! you won't 'eed nothin' else
But them spicy garlic smells,
An' the sunshine an' the palm-trees an' the
tinkly temple-bells;
On the road to Mandalay, etc.

I am sick o' wastin' leather on these gritty pavin'-stones,
An' the blasted Henglish drizzle wakes the fever in my bones;
Tho' I walks with fifty 'ousemaids outer Chelsea to the Strand,
An' they talks a lot o' lovin', but wot do they understand?
Beefy face an' grubby 'and—
Law! wot do they understand?

I've a neater, sweeter maiden in a cleaner,
greener land! On the road to Mandalay, etc.

Ship me somewheres east of Suez, where the best is like the worst,
Where there aren't no Ten Commandments an' a man can raise a thirst;
For the temple-bells are callin', and it's there that I would be—
By the old Moulmein Pagoda, looking lazy at the sea;

On the road to Mandalay,
Where the old Flotilla lay,
With our sick beneath the awnings when we
went to Mandalay!
Oh the road to Mandalay,
Where the flyin'-fishes play,
An' the dawn comes up like thunder outer
China 'crost the Bay!

TROOPIN'

(OUR ARMY IN THE EAST)

TROOPIN', troopin', troopin' to the sea:
'Ere's September come again—the six-year men are free.
O leave the dead be'ind us, for they cannot come Away
To where the ship's a-coalin' up that takes us 'ome to-day.

We're goin' 'ome, we're goin' 'ome,
Our ship is at the shore,
An' you must pack your 'aversack,
For we won't come back no more.
Ho, don't you grieve for me,
My lovely Mary-Ann,
For I'll marry you yit on a fourp'ny bit
As a time-expired man!

The Malabar's in 'arbour with the Jumner at 'er tail,
An' the time-expired's waitin' of 'is orders for to sail
Ho! the weary waitin' when on Khyber 'ills we lay,
But the time-expired's waitin' of 'is orders 'ome to-day.

They'll turn us out at Portsmouth wharf in cold an' wet an' rain,
All wearin' Injian cotton kit, but we will not com-plain;
They'll kill us of pneumonia—for that's their little way—
But damn the chills and fever, men, we're goin' 'ome to-day!

Troopin', troopin', winter's round again!
See the new draf's pourin' in for the old campaign;
Ho, you poor recruities, but you've got to earn your pay—
What's the last from Lunnon, lads? We're goin' there to-day.

Troopin', troopin', give another cheer—
'Ere's to English women an' a quart of English beer;

The Colonel an' the regiment an' all who've got to stay,
Gawd's mercy strike 'em gentle—Whoop! we're goin' 'ome to-day,

We're goin' 'ome, we're goin' 'ome,
Our ship is at the shore,
An' you must pack your 'aversack,
For we won't come back no more.
Ho, don't you grieve for me,
My lovely Mary-Ann,
For I'll marry you yit on a fourp'ny bit
As a time-expired man.

THE WIDOW'S PARTY

'WHERE have you been this while away,
Johnnie, Johnnie?'
Out with the rest on a picnic lay,
Johnnie, my Johnnie, aha !
They called us out of the barrack-yard
To Gawd knows where from Gosport Hard,
And you can't refuse when you get the card,
And the Widow gives the party.
(**Bugle.**) Ta—rara—ra-ra-rara!

'What did you get to eat and drink,
Johnnie, Johnnie?'
Standing water as thick as ink,
Johnnie, my Johnnie, aha!
A bit o' beef that were three year stored,
A bit o' mutton as tough as a board,
And a fowl we killed with a sergeant's sword,
When the Widow give the party.

'What did you do for knives and forks,
Johnnie, Johnnie?'
We carries 'em with us wherever we walks,
Johnnie, my Johnnie, aha!
And some was sliced and some was halved,
And some was crimped and some was carved,
And some was gutted and some was starved,
When the Widow give the party.

'What ha' you done with half your mess,

Johnnie, Johnnie?'
They couldn't do more and they wouldn't do less,
Johnnie, my Johnnie, aha!
They ate their whack and they drank their fill,
And I think the rations has made them ill,
For half my comp'ny's lying still
Where the Widow give the party.
'How did you get away—away,
Johnnie, Johnnie?'
On the broad o' my back at the end o' the day,
Johnnie, my Johnnie, aha!

I comed away like a bleedin' toff,
For I got four niggers to carry me off,
As I lay in the bight of a canvas trough,
When the Widow give the party.

'What was the end of all the show,
Johnnie, Johnnie?'
Ask my Colonel, for I don't know,
Johnnie, my Johnnie, aha!
We broke a King and we built a road—
A court-house stands where the reg'ment goed.
And the river's clean where the raw blood flowed
When the Widow give the party.
(***Bugle*** .) Ta—rara—ra-ra-rara!

FORD O' KABUL RIVER

KABUL town's by Kabul river—
Blow the bugle, draw the sword—
There I lef' my mate for ever,
Wet an' drippin' by the ford.

Ford, ford, ford o' Kabul river,
Ford o' Kabul river in the dark!
There's the river up and brimmin', an' there's
'arf a squadron swimmin'
'Cross the ford o' Kabul river in the dark.

Kabul town's a blasted place—
Blow the bugle, draw the sword—
'Strewth I shan't forget 'is face
Wet an' drippin' by the ford!
Ford, ford, ford o' Kabul river,
Ford o' Kabul river in the dark!
Keep the crossing-stakes beside you, an' they
 will surely guide you
'Cross the ford of Kabul river in the dark.

Kabul town is sun and dust—
Blow the bugle, draw the sword—
I'd ha' sooner drownded fust
'Stead of 'im beside the ford.
Ford, ford, ford o' Kabul river,
Ford o' Kabul river in the dark!
You can 'ear the 'orses threshing you can
'ear the men a-splashin',
'Cross the ford o' Kabul river in the dark.

Kabul town was ours to take—
Blow the bugle, draw the sword—.
I'd ha' left it for 'is sake—
'Im that left me by the ford.
Ford, ford, ford o' Kabul river,
Ford o' Kabul river in the dark!
It's none so bloomin' dry there; ain't you

never comin' nigh there,
'Cross the ford o' Kabul river in the dark?

Kabul town'll go to hell—
Blow the bugle, draw the sword—
'Fore I see him 'live an' well—
'Im the best beside the ford.

BARRACK-ROOM BALLADS

Ford, ford, ford o' Kabul river,
Ford o' Kabul river in the dark!
Gawd 'elp 'em if they blunder, for their
boots'll pull 'em under,
By the ford o' Kabul river in the dark.

Turn your 'orse from Kabul town—
 Blow the bugle, draw the sword—
'Im an' 'arf my troop is down,
Down an' drownded by the ford.
Ford, ford, ford o' Kabul river,
Ford o' Kabul river in the dark!
There's the river low an' fallin', but it ain't no use o' callin'
'Cross the ford o' Kabul river in the dark.

To the legion of the lost ones, to the cohort of the damned,
To my brethren in their sorrow overseas,
Sings a gentleman of England cleanly bred, machinely crammed,
And a trooper of the Empress, if you please.
Yea, a trooper of the forces who has run his own six horses,
And faith he went the pace and went it blind,
And the world was more than kin while he held the ready tin,
But to-day the Sergeant's something less than kind.

We're poor little lambs who've lost our way,
Baa! Baa! Baa!
We're little black sheep who've gone astray,
Baa—aa—aa!
Gentlemen-rankers out on the spree
Damned from here to Eternity,
God ha' mercy on such as we,
Baa! Yah! Bah!

Oh, it's sweet to sweat through stables, sweet to empty kitchen slops,
And it's sweet to hear the tales the troopers tell,
To dance with blowzy housemaids at the regimental hops,
And thrash the cad who says you waltz too well.
Yes, it makes you cock-a-hoop to be 'Rider' to your troop,
And branded with a blasted worsted spur,
When you envy, Oh, how keenly, one poor Tommy being cleanly
Who blacks your boots and sometimes call you 'Sir.'

If the home we never write to, and the oaths we never keep,
And all we know most distant and most dear,
Across the snoring barrack-room return to break our sleep,
Can you blame us if we soak ourselves in beer?
When the drunken comrade mutters and the great guard-lantern gutters
And the horror of our fall is written plain,
Every secret, self-revealing on the aching white-washed ceiling,
Do you wonder that we drug ourselves from pain?

GENTLEMEN-RANKERS

We have done with Hope and Honour, we are lost to Love and Truth,
We are dropping down the ladder rung by rung,
And the measure of our torment is the measure of our youth.
God help us, for we knew the worst too young!

Our shame is clean repentance for the crime that brought the sentence,
Our pride it is to know no spur of pride,
And the Curse of Reuben holds us till an alien turf enfolds us
And we die, and none can tell Them where we died.
We're poor little lambs who've lost our way,
Baa! Baa! Baa!
We're little black sheep who've gone astray,
Baa—aa—aa!
Gentlemen-rankers out on the spree,
Damned from here to Eternity,
God ha' mercy on such as we,
Baa! Yah! Bah!

ROUTE MARCHIN'

WE'RE marchin' on relief over Injia's sunny plains,
A little front o' Christmas time an' just be'ind the Rains,
Ho! get away, you bullock-man, you've 'eard the bugle blowed,
There's a regiment a-comin' down the Grand Trunk Road;
With its best foot first
And the road a-sliding past,
An' every bloomin' campin' -ground exactly
like the last;
While the Big Drum says,
With 'is ' rowdy-dowdy-dow!'—
'*Kiko kissywarsti don't you hamsher argyjow?*'

Oh, there's them Injian temples to admire when you see,
There's the peacock round the corner an' the monkey up the tree,
An' there's that rummy silver grass a-wavin' in the wind,
An' the old Grand Trunk a trailin' like a rifle-sling be'ind.
While it's best foot first, etc.

At half-past five's Revelly, an' our tents they down must come,
Like a lot of button mushrooms when you pick 'em up at 'ome.
But it's over in a minute, an' at six the column starts,
While the women and the kiddies sit an' shiver in the carts.
And it's best foot first, etc.

Oh, then it's open order, an' we lights our pipes an' sings,
An' we talks about our rations an' a lot of other things,
And we thinks o' friends in England, an' we wonders
what they're at, An' 'ow they would admire for to hear us sling the bat.[7]
An' it's best foot first, etc.

> [7] Thomas's first and firmest conviction is that he is a profound Orientalist
> and a fluent speaker of Hindustani. As a matter of feet, he depends largely
> on the sign-language.

It's none so bad o' Sunday, when you're lyin' at your ease,
To watch the kites a-wheelin' round them feather-'eaded trees,
For although there ain't no women yet there ain't no barrick-yards,
So the orficers goes shootin' an' the men they plays at cards.
Till it's best foot first, etc.

So 'ark an' 'eed you rookies, which is always grum-blin' sore,
There's worser things than marchin' from Umballa to Cawnpore;
And if your 'eels are blistered an' they feels to 'urt like 'ell
You drop some tallow in your socks an' that will make 'em well.
For it's best foot first, etc.

We're marchin' on relief over Injia's coral strand,
Eight 'undred fightin' Englishmen, the Colonel, and
the Band.

Ho! get away, you bullock-man, you've 'eard the bugle blowed,

There's a regiment a-comin' down the Grand Trunk Road.
With its best foot first
And the road a-sliding past,
An' every bloomin' campin'-ground exactly like the last;
While the Big Drum says, With 'is 'rowdy-dowdy-dow!'— ' Kikokissywarsti
don't you hamsherargyjaw?' [8]

[8] Why don't you get on ?

SHILLIN' A DAY

MY name is O'Kelly, I've heard the Revelly
From Birr to Bareilly, from Leeds to Lahore,
Hong-Kong and Peshawur,
Lucknow and Etawah,
And fifty-five more all endin' in 'pore.'
Black Death and his quickness, the depth and the
thickness, Of sorrow and sickness I've known on my way,
But I'm old and I'm nervis,
I'm cast from the Service,
And all I deserve is a shillin' a day.
(Chorus.) Shillin' a day
Bloomin' good pay—
Lucky to touch it, a shillin' a day!

Oh, it drives me half crazy to think of the days I
Went slap for the Ghazi my sword at my side,

When we rode Hell-for-leather
Both squadrons together,
That didn't care whether we lived or we died.
But it's no use desparin', my wife must go charm'

An' me commissairin' the pay-bills to better,
So if me you be'old
In the wet and the cold,
By the Grand Metropold won't you give me a letter?
(**Full Chorus** .) Give 'im a letter-
Can't do no better
Late Troop-Sergeant Major an'—runs
with a letter!
Think what 'e's been,
Think what 'e's seen,
Think of his pension an'

GAWD SAVE THE QUEEN !

L'ENVOI

THERE'S a whisper down the field where the year has shot her yield,
And the ricks stand grey to the sun,
Singing:—'Over then, come over, for the bee has quit the clover,
And your English summer's done.'
You have heard the beat of the off-shore wind,
And the thresh of the deep-sea rain;
You have heard the song—how long! how long?
Pull out on the trail again!

Ha' done with the Tents of Shem, dear lass,
We've seen the seasons through,
And it's time to turn on the old trail, our own trail, the out trail,
Pull out, pull out, on the Long Trail—the trail that is always new.

It's North you may run to the rime-ringed sun

Or South to the blind Horn's hate;
Or East all the way into Mississippi Bay,
Or West to the Golden Gate;

Where the blindest bluffs hold good, dear lass,
And the wildest tales are true,
And the men bulk big on the old trail, our own trail, the out trail,
And life runs large on the Long Trail—the trail that is always new.

The days are sick and cold, and the skies are grey and old,
And the twice-breathed airs blow damp;
And I'd sell my tired soul for the bucking beam-sea roll
Of a black Bilbao tramp;

With her load-line over her hatch, dear lass,
And a drunken Dago crew,
And her nose held down on the old trail, our own trail, the out trail
From Cadiz Bar on the Long Trail—the trail that is always new.

There be triple ways to take, of the eagle or the snake,
Or the way of a man with a maid;
But the sweetest way to me is a ship's upon the sea
In the heel of the North-East Trade.

Can you hear the crash on her bows, dear lass,
And the drum of the racing screw,
As she ships it green on the old trail, our own trail, the out trail,
As she lifts and 'scends on the Long Trail—thetrail that is always new?

See the shaking funnels roar, with the Peter at the fore,
And the fenders grind and heave,
And the derricks clack and grate as the tackle hooks the crate,
And the fall-rope whines through the sheave;

It's 'Gang-plank up and in,' dear lass,
It's 'Hawsers warp her through!'
And it's 'All clear aft' on the old trail, our own trail, the out trail,
We're backing down on the Long Trail—the trail that is always new.

Oh, the mutter overside, when the port-fog holds us tied,
And the syrens,hoot their dread!
When foot by foot we creep o'er the hueless viewless Deep
To the sob of the questing lead!
It's down by the Lower Hope, dear lass,
With the Gunfleet Sands in view,
Till the Mouse swings green on the old trail, our own trail, the out trail,
And the Gull Light lifts on the Long Trail—
the trail that is always new.

Oh, the blazing tropic night, when the wake's a welt of light
That holds the hot sky tame,
And the steady fore-foot snores through the planet-powdered floors
Where the scared whale flukes in flame!
Her plates are scarred by the sun, dear lass,
Her ropes are taunt with the dew,
For we're booming down on the old trail, our own trail, the out trail,
We're sagging south on the Long Trail—the trail that is always new.

Then home, get her home where the drunken rollers comb,
And the shouting seas drive by,
And the engines stamp and ring and the wet bows reel and swing,
And the Southern Cross rides high!

Yes, the old lost stars wheel back, dear lass,
That blaze in the velvet blue.
They're all old friends on the old trail, our own trail, the out trail,
They're God's own guides on the Long Trail—

the trail that is always new.

Fly forward, O my heart, from the Foreland to the Start—
We're steaming all too slow,
And it's twenty thousand miles to our little lazy isle
Where the trumpet-orchids blow!

You have heard the call of the off-shore wind
And the voice of the deep-sea rain—
You have heard the song—how long! how long?
Pull out on the trail again!

The Lord knows what we may find, dear lass,
And the Deuce knows what we may do—
But we're back once more on the old trail, our own trail, the out trail,
We're down, hull-down on the Long Trail—the trail that is always new.

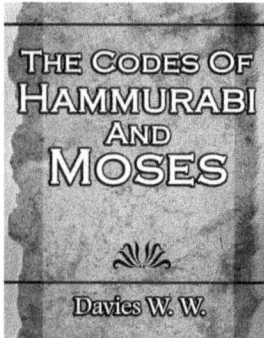

The Codes Of Hammurabi And Moses
W. W. Davies

QTY

The discovery of the Hammurabi Code is one of the greatest achievements of archaeology, and is of paramount interest, not only to the student of the Bible, but also to all those interested in ancient history...

Religion   **ISBN:** *1-59462-338-4*   Pages:132

MSRP $12.95

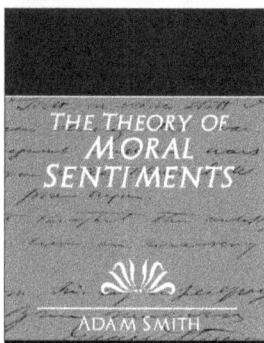

The Theory of Moral Sentiments
Adam Smith

QTY

This work from 1749. contains original theories of conscience amd moral judgment and it is the foundation for systemof morals.

Philosophy **ISBN:** *1-59462-777-0*   Pages:536

MSRP $19.95

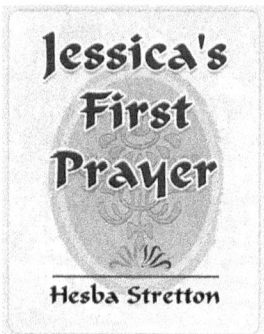

Jessica's First Prayer
Hesba Stretton

QTY

In a screened and secluded corner of one of the many railway-bridges which span the streets of London there could be seen a few years ago, from five o'clock every morning until half past eight, a tidily set-out coffee-stall, consisting of a trestle and board, upon which stood two large tin cans, with a small fire of charcoal burning under each so as to keep the coffee boiling during the early hours of the morning when the work-people were thronging into the city on their way to their daily toil...

Pages:84

Childrens   **ISBN:** *1-59462-373-2*   *MSRP $9.95*

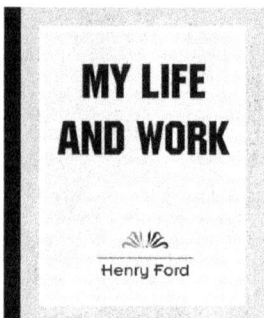

My Life and Work
Henry Ford

QTY

Henry Ford revolutionized the world with his implementation of mass production for the Model T automobile. Gain valuable business insight into his life and work with his own auto-biography... "We have only started on our development of our country we have not as yet, with all our talk of wonderful progress, done more than scratch the surface. The progress has been wonderful enough but..."

Pages:300

Biographies/   **ISBN:** *1-59462-198-5*   *MSRP $21.95*

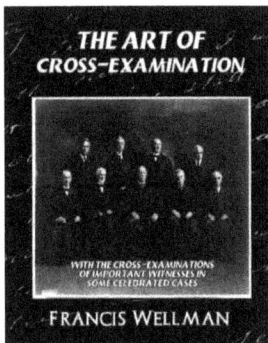

The Art of Cross-Examination
Francis Wellman

QTY

I presume it is the experience of every author, after his first book is published upon an important subject, to be almost overwhelmed with a wealth of ideas and illustrations which could readily have been included in his book, and which to his own mind, at least, seem to make a second edition inevitable. Such certainly was the case with me; and when the first edition had reached its sixth impression in five months, I rejoiced to learn that it seemed to my publishers that the book had met with a sufficiently favorable reception to justify a second and considerably enlarged edition. ..

Reference   ISBN: *1-59462-647-2*

Pages:412

MSRP $19.95

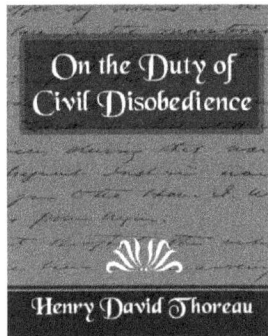

On the Duty of Civil Disobedience
Henry David Thoreau

QTY

Thoreau wrote his famous essay, On the Duty of Civil Disobedience, as a protest against an unjust but popular war and the immoral but popular institution of slave-owning. He did more than write—he declined to pay his taxes, and was hauled off to gaol in consequence. Who can say how much this refusal of his hastened the end of the war and of slavery ?

Law   ISBN: *1-59462-747-9*

Pages:48

MSRP $7.45

Dream Psychology Psychoanalysis for Beginners
Sigmund Freud

QTY

Sigmund Freud, born Sigismund Schlomo Freud (May 6, 1856 - September 23, 1939), was a Jewish-Austrian neurologist and psychiatrist who co-founded the psychoanalytic school of psychology. Freud is best known for his theories of the unconscious mind, especially involving the mechanism of repression; his redefinition of sexual desire as mobile and directed towards a wide variety of objects; and his therapeutic techniques, especially his understanding of transference in the therapeutic relationship and the presumed value of dreams as sources of insight into unconscious desires.

Psychology   ISBN: *1-59462-905-6*

Pages:196

MSRP $15.45

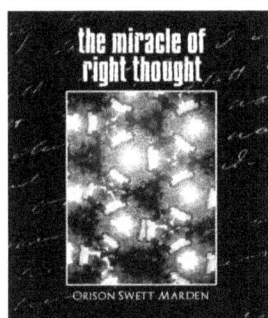

The Miracle of Right Thought
Orison Swett Marden

QTY

Believe with all of your heart that you will do what you were made to do. When the mind has once formed the habit of holding cheerful, happy, prosperous pictures, it will not be easy to form the opposite habit. It does not matter how improbable or how far away this realization may see, or how dark the prospects may be, if we visualize them as best we can, as vividly as possible, hold tenaciously to them and vigorously struggle to attain them, they will gradually become actualized, realized in the life. But a desire, a longing without endeavor, a yearning abandoned or held indifferently will vanish without realization.

Pages:360

Self Help   ISBN: *1-59462-644-8*

MSRP $25.45

QTY

The Rosicrucian Cosmo-Conception Mystic Christianity by *Max Heindel* ISBN: *1-59462-188-8* **$38.95**
The Rosicrucian Cosmo-conception is not dogmatic, neither does it appeal to any other authority than the reason of the student. It is: not controversial, but is: sent forth in the, hope that it may help to clear... New Age/Religion Pages 646

Abandonment To Divine Providence by *Jean-Pierre de Caussade* ISBN: *1-59462-228-0* **$25.95**
"The Rev. Jean Pierre de Caussade was one of the most remarkable spiritual writers of the Society of Jesus in France in the 18th Century. His death took place at Toulouse in 1751. His works have gone through many editions and have been republished... Inspirational/Religion Pages 400

Mental Chemistry by *Charles Haanel* ISBN: *1-59462-192-6* **$23.95**
Mental Chemistry allows the change of material conditions by combining and appropriately utilizing the power of the mind. Much like applied chemistry creates something new and unique out of careful combinations of chemicals the mastery of mental chemistry... New Age Pages 354

The Letters of Robert Browning and Elizabeth Barret Barrett 1845-1846 vol II ISBN: *1-59462-193-4* **$35.95**
by *Robert Browning* and *Elizabeth Barrett* Biographies Pages 596

Gleanings In Genesis (volume I) by *Arthur W. Pink* ISBN: *1-59462-130-6* **$27.45**
Appropriately has Genesis been termed "the seed plot of the Bible" for in it we have, in germ form, almost all of the great doctrines which are afterwards fully developed in the books of Scripture which follow... Religion/Inspirational Pages 420

The Master Key by *L. W. de Laurence* ISBN: *1-59462-001-6* **$30.95**
In no branch of human knowledge has there been a more lively increase of the spirit of research during the past few years than in the study of Psychology, Concentration and Mental Discipline. The requests for authentic lessons in Thought Control, Mental Discipline and... New Age/Business Pages 422

The Lesser Key Of Solomon Goetia by *L. W. de Laurence* ISBN: *1-59462-092-X* **$9.95**
This translation of the first book of the "Lernegton" which is now for the first time made accessible to students of Talismanic Magic was done, after careful collation and edition, from numerous Ancient Manuscripts in Hebrew, Latin, and French... New Age/Occult Pages 92

Rubaiyat Of Omar Khayyam by *Edward Fitzgerald* ISBN:*1-59462-332-5* **$13.95**
Edward Fitzgerald, whom the world has already learned, in spite of his own efforts to remain within the shadow of anonymity, to look upon as one of the rarest poets of the century, was born at Bredfield, in Suffolk, on the 31st of March, 1809. He was the third son of John Purcell... Music Pages 172

Ancient Law by *Henry Maine* ISBN: *1-59462-128-4* **$29.95**
The chief object of the following pages is to indicate some of the earliest ideas of mankind, as they are reflected in Ancient Law, and to point out the relation of those ideas to modern thought. Religion/History Pages 452

Far-Away Stories by *William J. Locke* ISBN: *1-59462-129-2* **$19.45**
"Good wine needs no bush, but a collection of mixed vintages does. And this book is just such a collection. Some of the stories I do not want to remain buried for ever in the museum files of dead magazine-numbers an author's not unpardonable vanity..." Fiction Pages 272

Life of David Crockett by *David Crockett* ISBN: *1-59462-250-7* **$27.45**
"Colonel David Crockett was one of the most remarkable men of the times in which he lived. Born in humble life, but gifted with a strong will, an indomitable courage, and unremitting perseverance... Biographies/New Age Pages 424

Lip-Reading by *Edward Nitchie* ISBN: *1-59462-206-X* **$25.95**
Edward B. Nitchie, founder of the New York School for the Hard of Hearing, now the Nitchie School of Lip-Reading, Inc, wrote "LIP-READING Principles and Practice". The development and perfecting of this meritorious work on lip-reading was an undertaking... How-to Pages 400

A Handbook of Suggestive Therapeutics, Applied Hypnotism, Psychic Science ISBN: *1-59462-214-0* **$24.95**
by *Henry Munro* Health/New Age/Health/Self-help Pages 376

A Doll's House: and Two Other Plays by *Henrik Ibsen* ISBN: *1-59462-112-8* **$19.95**
Henrik Ibsen created this classic when in revolutionary 1848 Rome. Introducing some striking concepts in playwriting for the realist genre, this play has been studied the world over. Fiction/Classics/Plays 308

The Light of Asia by *sir Edwin Arnold* ISBN: *1-59462-204-3* **$13.95**
In this poetic masterpiece, Edwin Arnold describes the life and teachings of Buddha. The man who was to become known as Buddha to the world was born as Prince Gautama of India but he rejected the worldly riches and abandoned the reigns of power when... Religion/History/Biographies Pages 170

The Complete Works of Guy de Maupassant by *Guy de Maupassant* ISBN: *1-59462-157-8* **$16.95**
"For days and days, nights and nights, I had dreamed of that first kiss which was to consecrate our engagement, and I knew not on what spot I should put my lips..." Fiction/Classics Pages 240

The Art of Cross-Examination by *Francis L. Wellman* ISBN: *1-59462-309-0* **$26.95**
Written by a renowned trial lawyer, Wellman imparts his experience and uses case studies to explain how to use psychology to extract desired information through questioning. How-to/Science/Reference Pages 408

Answered or Unanswered? by *Louisa Vaughan* ISBN: *1-59462-248-5* **$10.95**
Miracles of Faith in China Religion Pages 112

The Edinburgh Lectures on Mental Science (1909) by *Thomas* ISBN: *1-59462-008-3* **$11.95**
This book contains the substance of a course of lectures recently given by the writer in the Queen Street Hall, Edinburgh. Its purpose is to indicate the Natural Principles governing the relation between Mental Action and Material Conditions... New Age/Psychology Pages 148

Ayesha by *H. Rider Haggard* ISBN: *1-59462-301-5* **$24.95**
Verily and indeed it is the unexpected that happens! Probably if there was one person upon the earth from whom the Editor of this, and of a certain previous history, did not expect to hear again... Classics Pages 380

Ayala's Angel by *Anthony Trollope* ISBN: *1-59462-352-X* **$29.95**
The two girls were both pretty, but Lucy who was twenty-one who supposed to be simple and comparatively unattractive, whereas Ayala was credited, as her Bombwhat romantic name might show, with poetic charm and a taste for romance. Ayala when her father died was nineteen... Fiction Pages 484

The American Commonwealth by *James Bryce* ISBN: *1-59462-286-8* **$34.45**
An interpretation of American democratic political theory. It examines political mechanics and society from the perspective of Scotsman James Bryce Politics Pages 572

Stories of the Pilgrims by *Margaret P. Pumphrey* ISBN: *1-59462-116-0* **$17.95**
This book explores pilgrims religious oppression in England as well as their escape to Holland and eventual crossing to America on the Mayflower, and their early days in New England... History Pages 268

www.bookjungle.com *email: sales@bookjungle.com fax: 630-214-0564 mail: Book Jungle PO Box 2226 Champaign, IL 61825*

QTY

The Fasting Cure *by Sinclair Upton*   ISBN: *1-59462-222-1* $13.95
In the Cosmopolitan Magazine for May, 1910, and in the Contemporary Review (London) for April, 1910, I published an article dealing with my experiences in fasting. I have written a great many magazine articles, but never one which attracted so much attention... New Age/Self Help/Health Pages 164

Hebrew Astrology *by Sepharial*   ISBN: *1-59462-308-2* $13.45
In these days of advanced thinking it is a matter of common observation that we have left many of the old landmarks behind and that we are now pressing forward to greater heights and to a wider horizon than that which represented the mind-content of our progenitors... Astrology Pages 144

Thought Vibration or The Law of Attraction in the Thought World   ISBN: *1-59462-127-6* $12.95

by William Walker Atkinson   Psychology/Religion Pages 144

Optimism *by Helen Keller*   ISBN: *1-59462-108-X* $15.95
Helen Keller was blind, deaf, and mute since 19 months old, yet famously learned how to overcome these handicaps, communicate with the world, and spread her lectures promoting optimism. An inspiring read for everyone... Biographies/Inspirational Pages 84

Sara Crewe *by Frances Burnett*   ISBN: *1-59462-360-0* $9.45
In the first place, Miss Minchin lived in London. Her home was a large, dull, tall one, in a large, dull square, where all the houses were alike, and all the sparrows were alike, and where all the door-knockers made the same heavy sound... Childrens/Classic Pages 88

The Autobiography of Benjamin Franklin *by Benjamin Franklin*   ISBN: *1-59462-135-7* $24.95
The Autobiography of Benjamin Franklin has probably been more extensively read than any other American historical work, and no other book of its kind has had such ups and downs of fortune. Franklin lived for many years in England, where he was agent... Biographies/History Pages 332

Name	
Email	
Telephone	
Address	
City, State ZIP	

☐ **Credit Card**   ☐ **Check / Money Order**

Credit Card Number	
Expiration Date	
Signature	

Please Mail to: Book Jungle
PO Box 2226
Champaign, IL 61825
or Fax to: 630-214-0564

ORDERING INFORMATION

web*: www.bookjungle.com*
email*: sales@bookjungle.com*
fax*: 630-214-0564*
mail*: Book Jungle PO Box 2226 Champaign, IL 61825*
or PayPal *to sales@bookjungle.com*

Please contact us for bulk discounts

DIRECT-ORDER TERMS

**20% Discount if You Order
Two or More Books**
Free Domestic Shipping!
Accepted: Master Card, Visa,
Discover, American Express

www.ingramcontent.com/pod-product-compliance
Lightning Source LLC
Chambersburg PA
CBHW081233090426
42738CB00016B/3291